In years past a successful business owner or manager, only needed to focus on the key elements of customer satisfaction, developing new products to generate growth and controlling costs to optimize share holder value. In more recent times the elements of work place safety and environmental protection were added to the list. One important characteristic of these elements is their ability to be measured, providing business leaders both historical trend analysis and leading indicators to accurately predict future business performance and make well informed management decisions.

In today's environment, business leaders are challenged with a new element, human behavior, an element no so easily measured, more difficult to predict and more challenging to manage. Life Rage provides the reader an opportunity to explore the new frontier of human behavior, its importance in to days business environment and offers guidance for business leaders of the 21st century to successfully manage the element of human behavior and continue on their path to success.

H. L. Musler
Director Corporate Security
Ferro Corporation

Life Rage is a fascinating examination of our society. It provides much thought provoking information in a sensible and objective manner.

Roger E. Herman,
Strategic Business Futurist, Author, Speaker, Fellow,
The Institute of Management Consultants

Dimoff continues to prove his position as the pre-eminent workplace security professional in the United States.
His work combines thoughtful insights, creative solutions and sound advice.

David J. Akers,
President of EagleCheck, Ltd.

# LIFE RAGE

# LIFE RAGE

*AMERICA'S NEW MILLENNIUM*

TIMOTHY A. DIMOFF

To order additional copies of this book, contact:
Xlibris Corporation
1-888-795-4274
www.Xlibris.com
Orders@Xlibris.com
18632

# CONTENTS

*This book is dedicated
to every person in our society
who is trying to do his or her individual part
in reducing and eliminating any form of rage in our daily lives.*

*A special thanks to my wife, Michelle, and my three children,
Jenny, Danielle and Darrin for allowing me the time to research
and write this important book.*
*Additionally, I would like to offer my sincere gratitude
to several people who assisted in making this book a success:
Katina Jones, Kathy Baker, Cindy Grahl, Carol Mart Saferin,
Sam Lombardo, Father Norm Douglas and Karen Cimini.*

## Foreword

When I was much younger and at the beginning of my career as a psychologist, I studied and worked with a man who taught me that something we valued had to be backed up either by action or by money or it really wasn't valuable to us. At that time in my life, I argued the point. I said that there were many things I valued that I had no time or money to give to, and he responded that if that was so, then they were not really important to me. Today, after 20 years of living and working with other people's problems and issues, I know with certainty that he was right. If we truly value an idea or a person or a thing, we put time and/or money into them.

Tim Dimoff, the author of this book, is a man who understands and acts on this concept in every facet of his life. He consistently puts time and resources into his teaching, his writing, his work, his family and his community. He is a supporter and activist in the things he believes in passionately, and even more importantly, supports and encourages passion and commitment in those around him.

Tim sees "life rage" in the world around him and, as a former police officer, has experienced some of the worst of it first-hand. While the theorists spend time trying to figure out the "whys" of this anger, Tim offers some concrete ideas of what to do about it. He recognizes that there is an interconnection to these problems, and explores life rage at the family, community, corporate, and governmental levels. He also examines media and technology, and makes some suggestions about their contributions to human isolation and anger.

This is a book written by a layperson, for the layperson. As such, it is not written in statistic-heavy societal analysis, but rather in an accessible common language we can all relate to and understand. *Life Rage* is a useable guide toward changing our own lives and leaving the world a better place than we found it—a worthy goal for all of us.

Karen T. Cimini, Ph.D.
Akron Family Institute, Akron, Ohio

**Chapter I**

# LIFE RAGE: THE PROBLEM—SOCIETY ON THE EDGE

What is America? It is ripped from the pages of our newspapers and read in our headlines. Road rage. Marital frustration. Stalking. Aggressive travelers. Frustration with health care. Workplace violence. Sexual abuse. Racial and religious intolerance. Disrespectful kids. Rude clerks. Terrorism. Litigiousness. Mounting use of illegal drugs. Disdain for government. The militia movement. Harassment. Kids killing kids. And the list goes on. Altogether, we call it life rage.

It was supposed to be so different. Life's journey is supposed to be an enjoyable marathon, but America has turned it into a sprint. We tell our children, employees and citizens to stop and smell the roses, but we provide them with a contradictory controlled environment that is an incubator of speed at all costs in our homes, work environments and society in general.

What's going on? It seems that everywhere we turn, frustrations are spilling over. Life in America today is not what we had hoped for, and it is causing rage. It is the best of times; it is the worst of times. We have taller buildings, but shorter tempers. Wider freeways, but narrower viewpoints. We spend more but have less. We buy more but enjoy it less. We drink and eat too much, spend too recklessly, laugh too little, get angry too quickly, get up too tired, read too seldom and watch too much TV. We've added years to our lives, but not life to our years.

Let's call it Life Rage, this establishment of irrational behavior as the norm in every area of human experience. Are we the angriest society on earth? I think so. America is number one in all the wrong categories. We have more incidents of murder, violent crimes, divorces, abortion, teen suicide, cocaine consumption, sexually transmitted diseases, pornography production, kids killing kids, than any civilized nation in the world, and that's a fact.

We have riots in the streets primarily along racial and economic lines that are spurred by a simple jury verdict. We cannot even have a jury verdict without repercussions. We have low-intensity warfare, domestic terrorism, and irrational behavior established as the norm in every area of human experience. In sports. In school. In the home.

The statistics are frightening. Throughout this book, we will begin by providing these statistics to show you the scope of the problem, and then we will explore the reasons behind those statistics, the factors that caused them to develop. Finally, in each chapter and in the book as a whole, we will outline some possible solutions to the problem of America's duel with Life Rage.

- *Let's begin with drugs.* The *United States consumes 60% of all the world's illegally produced drugs, while we are only 6% of the total population.* That is startling. Does it mean that most Americans are illegal drug users? Absolutely not. We have about 20 million drug users in this country out of our entire population. But we do have the highest per capita income, the biggest amount of money in the world. And drug dealers are attracted to money.

Heroin is making a fast comeback because of the change in the drug perception in the world. It used to be 4% pure a decade ago and you needed to inject it into your body with a needle. Now you can buy heroin on the street at 50% to 70% purity, and you can snort it, eat it, blast it—whatever. Our accommodating neighbors in South and Central America are tearing out their coca fields and planting heroin-producing plants in order to meet the increasing U.S. demand.

My company specializes in drug testing programs for a drug-free workplace, and I get companies debating whether they should have such a program. Not only should they, but they should have a drug testing program that supports an employee-assistance program so that when you do uncover problems, you can help that worker, that social being, get help. If they do get help, they can do better. We have found that the most effective drug treatment programs are not the professional treatment facilities and the like but the programs provided and supported by employers. Why? The support of the employer and the family together helps people recover and stay clean, and workers have great motivation to succeed. But they need that hand extended first by the company in order to get into the program.

Drug abuse is not caused by peer pressure, but by negativity and low self-esteem. Helping to build self-esteem up in both employees and children is a great way to fight drugs.

• *One out of every 20 people in the United States will serve time in prison with a record number on probation.* People are now saying that crime is down. It is down partly because we have jailed more people than ever in the history of the United States, built a record number of additional prisons and placed a higher number of people on probation and parole.

The other reason is that in 1995, the federal government changed the way it kept crime statistics. Before that, if someone committed three crimes in one location, it counted as three crimes, but now they can count as one. Statistics can say whatever you want, but I doubt if crime is really down. And what do we do when we bring the people out of jail? Are we training them in prison for them to be able to commit more crime or rehabilitating them?

One of the tests of a civilization is to provide swift, sure and fair justice to all citizens in order to protect the social order and its citizens. But the rate of violent crime increased more than 520% in just over three years, with teen drug arrests rising 1,451% since 1965. In 1994, the prison population grew by 1,600 people a week. This makes the justice system overloaded, and rehab has to become a forgotten dream. It also means people lose faith in the justice system as criminals avoid conviction because of legalisms and convoluted defense systems.

- *From 1960-1991, the U.S. population increased by 40%, but violent crime rose 500%, murders 170%, rapes 520%, assaults 600%.* One of every 50 kids has a parent in prison. There's more: for people 15 to 24 years of age, murder is the second leading cause of death, and for African-Americas, it leads.

- *When it comes to kids killing other kids with guns, you can take the number of kids who did that in all the civilized countries in the world just two years ago, add them together and multiply them by 10, and you would not equal the number of kids in the U.S. who killed other kids with guns.* There were 5,285 kids who killed kids with guns in the U.S. two years ago. From 1984 to 1994, firearm death rates increased 222% for kids from 15-to 19-year age bracket. For every child killed by a gun, four are wounded. Guns are expected to take over motor vehicles as the leading cause of death within five years for American children.

I am not speaking against guns. I do not think that the right to bear arms is a factor. Rage is instead a factor of attitude. In America, guns are just part of a whole problem of a bad attitude.

Take Switzerland, for instance. In Switzerland, when you are 16, you must own a gun, and you must go to school to learn to use it. And they do not have problems with guns. On the flip side, when Hitler was invading Europe during World War II, he said that there was one country that Germany would not invade: Switzerland. When his general asked him why, he said that everyone at age 16 and older was required to have a gun.

In 1972, the Consumer Product Safety Commission was formed to regulate every product in the United States, except one. Firearms. A squirt gun has more regulation than a Magnum 44. There are things that can be done to make guns safer to have around our homes and in our daily lives.

The sniper incident in Washington, D.C., is another new type of day-to-day violence that we Americans now have to live with, and most likely there will be more "creative" terrorism acts in the future. The U.S. is slowly becoming a large Israel where citizens will be forced to live daily with the thought of potential random violence against themselves, their family members, co-workers and the general public.

- *Each year one million victims are involved in workplace assaults.* The good news is that high-level incidents of violence in the workplace such as shootings are down. We have become sensitized to it and have gone to great lengths to make sure it doesn't happen. However, things such as employee-on-employee violence, harassment, and stalking have gone up tenfold. People just aren't getting along with each other anymore.

So, by the time you get to work, you are already upset. You drive to a convenience store for coffee and the person behind the counter is rude. The clerk doesn't care if you are a customer and buying things from her will provide her with job security. You leave, drive down the road, someone sticks a finger in the air to let you know you are "number one" in their lives. You drive further, hit orange barrels, take a detour, and get to work already upset. The first person you see is still angry from his own trip in and gets into your face. By 8:45, you've had four rage encounters, and that's after leaving home. It's going to be a good day. You've got an overdemanding workload, fast-paced, multiple jobs, disciplinary actions, labor negotiations and layoffs caused by mergers and acquisitions. The negative encounters and day-to-day pressures are endless. Your days are long with no end in sight.

- *But 72% of the mergers and acquisitions in the last 12 years have been financial failures* at the cost of millions and millions and millions of jobs, with a resultant impact on families and communities. In the last six years, big business has gutted 4 million jobs, while small business has created 645,000 jobs in just one year. Representing approximately 84% of the economy, small business is the backbone of the domestic country and will continue to be so, especially as globalization makes its impact.

Small business can give us the warm fuzzies, but big business, like Starbucks, can learn to do this too. Their average customer comes back 17 times a month for one of the more expensive coffee in the world. You feel appreciated, and you feel like someone cares. The number one attribute workers are looking for is to be appreciated. It is also numbers two and three. Not money. Not benefits. I advise management in corporations that we need to change the tempo. One very effective solution I suggest is that every day, each manager, owner, supervisor, teacher, parent, and person should find someone who is doing something right and thank him or her. We can change the world if we conquer it one person at a time!

Example: When I go into a store and the clerks are having a bad day, I hand them free comedy club tickets, and tell them thanks to help brighten their day. The reaction is phenomenal, but it would be even better if the manager would come in and tell them thanks.

- *The average person in the workplace will have 10 different jobs and change of careers three times.* Right now, 60% of the workforce plans to change their job in the next 12 months. Three-quarters of employers are not happy working where they are. We do not even hang onto our customers more than a national average of four years, despite Starbuck's success rate.

Whatever happened to the idea that customer service equals customer retention? Start with employee satisfaction and appreciation. Customers want to work with reliable employees who can deliver a solid relationship.

Globalization will continue to impact us, large or small. Can small business underbid companies oversees who can do work for a great deal less? Will buyers continue to patronize nearby vendors when parts can be ordered from abroad and shipped here for substantially less? Of course, with a time factor involved and just-in-time manufacturing, it might be worth it to have the part sooner.

Corporate life takes us away from our kids as technology speed things up to 150 miles an hour. We wear 10 hats and work 12 hours and take stuff home. It is a rat race, and we do not even get to enjoy change. When I was growing up and a new cartoon came on, or a new toy came out, I got to enjoy it for a long time.

Today, there is a new toy every month or week. A few years ago, we were all playing with 486 computers and thinking it was great and now it's all Pentium driven. And then there are guys sitting in bed with a can of Pepsi and some Fritos creating viruses. I'd love to see software that can trace those guys back to their bedrooms so we can find them and punish them. But instead we glamorize them on the front page repeatedly and reward them.

- I*n 1980, CEO pay ratio to that of the average worker was 42 to one. In 1990, it was 85 to one. Now it is 484 to one.* And if they screw up, we give them millions of dollars to leave. Frank Blondi, Jr., fired from Universal Studies, got a severance package worth $30 million on top of the $15 million package he got when fired as CEO of Viacom. And former BankAmerica CEO David Coulter was dismissed, and drew a $5 million pension for life. We reward failure at our highest levels.

    In Japan, on the other hand, the CEO ratio pay can never be higher than eleven to one, so if a CEO wants to do better, he has to improve salaries for all and bring the average pay up.

    Look at former president Harry Truman and former GE head Jack Welch. Both were celebrated by Peter Drucker for their intellectual integrity, for taking on their jobs objectively, realizing that they were not their own master but rather the servants of the organization they headed, be it nation or corporation. They subordinated their own desires to the welfare of the institution.

    Overpayment for screwing up happens in professional sports, too, as players demand outrageous salaries and get them despite performance.

- *A national survey said that America has lost its manners, and that 79% of adults think it is a serious problem, while 61% think is has gotten worse.* Rudeness rules. We walk around with cell phones in our ears, curse in public loudly and habitually, not just because we stub a toe but as a matter of course. Poor customer service has caused half of us to leave a store without buying something. Six in ten drivers say they see others drive aggressively. These results were consistent geographically, and people blamed it on overcrowding and being too busy. We hear complaints about the speed of life, a plea to stop the merry-go-round, and various movements to a simpler lifestyle.

- *In sports, three out of five professional football players have rap sheets.* Athletes can choke coaches, spit on fans and punch referees and they still get to play. Fines are ludicrous. Players can say fans don't matter and still be popular. And so you have an NBA championship that is celebrating by turning over cruisers and setting fires, breaking windows and pillaging businesses.

- *By the age of thirteen, 70% of kids involved in sports drop out because it is no longer fun.* This is bad because a kid's coaches can be mentors, can be the final place for kids to learn what they did not learn at home or in the school—a direction in life. Sports are no longer about learning skills, learning teamwork, learning endurance, and having fun. It's a job, and not just for the pros, but for our younger kids.

- *Your child gets 1,000 hours in the classroom a year and 1,640 hours in front of the TV.* We should take the TVs out of all kid's bedrooms. Bedrooms are for sleeping and dressing. They are not clubhouses and putting TVs into them turns them into isolation chambers where kids can become alienated from the family. Computers should come out as well, so parents can monitor what is going on. Computers can bring a lot of unwelcome and unhealthy things into the home.

TVs take an average six hours a day from our kids to teach them that if you disagree with someone, you get rid of them; that sex with anyone at any time anywhere is OK; that music that advocates extreme violence is just fine; that graphic pictures of violence, rape, and torture are theirs for the asking, along with pornography; that disrespect for life is good; and that disrespect for authority is absolutely mandatory.

- *The average child sees 8,000 murders and 100,000 acts of violence on television before they graduate from grade school.* This has a big effect. And not just on the individual but on society as well. Why are there so many school shootings? What caused them to proliferate? It's called the copycat effect. When you put a 14-year-old on the front page of a news magazine and profile him 100 times a day on the televisions, you have glamorized him and made him a god in the eyes of the other kids.

  Other kids with problems see that with broken homes and stress, they do not only want to match but to outdo, to excel. In Japan, it is against the law to put any crime that a kid commits in any media format. The Japanese people know for a fact that it does not have a positive impact.

  Why are there more shootings in the workplace than there were 10 to 20 years ago? For the same reason. We provide a blueprint. We set the seeds of example. Irrational behavior is the acceptable way to go for people who are under stress. It's not all copycat, and there are other factors at work, but it is a big part of the problem.

- *Two-thirds of Americans eat dinner while watching TV.* We need to eat dinner together, maybe not every night but at least three or four times a week, without TV, so we can talk together. Dinnertime is communication, confession, and realization. It is where kids learn to talk, to listen and to debate. It is where you learn people skills. The best cultures—the stronger ones—eat dinner together. Period.

- *On average, a father communicates with a kid in a positive way about one minute a day, and a mother about seven minutes a day.* Some 28% of kids in this country live with a single parent. It is not broken homes and single parents, because if you have a single parent showering that child with love, that child will grow. It is the quality of the parenting. How much time do we spend parenting and being with our families?

For instance, there is the story of "Smoking Joe." I volunteer three times a year with the Christian Youth Organization that trains coaches on several aspects in hopes of better preparing them to influence our youth in a positive way. My assignment is to discuss with the coaches their role and influence in the dangers of alcohol and drug abuse. The coaches are always anticipating hearing the usual lecture on how alcohol and drugs are bad. But my presentation is about their importance as "role models" and how much influence they will have on each child's future attitude not only about drugs/alcohol, but everything, including work ethics, team building skills, crime, respect, character, etc.

During this presentation, I tell a true story about my 12 years experience of coaching 6-to18-year-old boys and girls. Once I was asked what my most rewarding experience in coaching was. Without hesitation, I talk about "Smoking Joe."

Joe was a shy young boy about nine years old who came from a divorced family. Joe lived with his mother and had lost quite a bit of self-esteem as a result of the divorce and unfortunate weak relationship with his father. Joe loved to play baseball, and, several days a week, would throw a rubber ball against the wall at the apartment, thinking to himself that he wanted to be a good baseball player. This desire revolved around one dream that his dad would come to watch him play. I did not know at the time, but after he was on my team, his mother clarified the situation for me. She said that Joe's dad would not come to watch his son play ball because Joe was not a starter on the previous teams he played on.

On draft day, none of the coaches wanted Joe because of his lack of talent. I said I would take Joe. The first day I met Joe, he would not look up at me, so I stooped down on the ground and looked up at Joe and into his eyes when we talked.

After doing this quite a few times, Joe decided he would look at me when we talked, and I was able to stand up. I knew at this time that self-esteem was Joe's downfall and we needed to build it back up.

At practice, we worked with Joe, and one day it happened. I had a line of players on third base and asked them to throw the ball to first as hard as they could. When it was Joe's turn, I hit him the ball and he barely got the ball to first. I stopped and asked Joe to throw the ball as hard as he could to first and not to worry about where it went. Joe picked up the next grounder and fired it to first base. You could hear the crack in the mitt of the first baseman. I asked Joe to do it again. He fired the ball again to the first baseman and the child at first dropped his mitt and waved his aching hand in the air that was on fire.

I stopped in amazement and called all my players to the mound. I made an announcement that Joe was now the starting third baseman for this team. Additionally, I said there will be one *big* change. Joe would no longer be called "Joe." I announced that Joe's new name was "Smoking Joe." The look on Joe's face was worth a million dollars.

After practice, when Joe's mom came to pick him up, Joe ran across the park to his mother yelling out loud, "Mom, Mom! I have a new name!" His mother called me that night and said, "Thanks—I have never seen Joe so happy in years."

Joe went on to be a very good player, and yes, his dad now showed up to watch Joe play baseball. Some people say that I should be upset with the dad who finally decided to show up. I said no—I brought a father and son back together, and my negative thoughts would have no positive effect in this situation, so I decided to only focus on the good. My role as a coach is to build strong and positive self-esteem in our youth—not to judge.

Kids don't appreciate what we buy them or what sacrifices we make for them. They complain because we don't spend enough time with them. Kids are suffering from resource deprivation. They have no reliable sources for love, support and education. You love your child, but you also discipline him. You discipline him because you love him, humanely. Fifteen million kids are growing up unprepared for any kind of life except dependency and crime, or of not growing up at all.

We need to teach them to tear themselves away from the negative and reflect on the positive: that true character is what you do when no one is watching; to never, ever give in to irrational behavior.

How a kid feels about family, work, sex, education—his moral and ethical foundations—are 80% formed before the age of eight. In today's America, there is a negative attitude, and it sets the pace. Young people are increasingly pessimistic about marriage, according to the National Marriage Project, with the percentage of high school girls who expect to stay married for life dropping 64% in 1995. Fifty-three percent says it's okay to have a child out of wedlock, vs. 33% in 1976. Today's kids are not getting moral guidance in the home anymore. Then they go to school, and we beg our teachers to straighten them out; but that is a tough job and improper request. A very tough job that takes time away from the reason why kids used to go to school—to learn to read and do math.

Don't let the distinction between right and wrong get blurred in your family's life. Do not hold onto the gray area. Where is religion in all of this? Where is God? Your leader? It is crazy not to allow prayer in school, allowing those who do not want to abstain. If you took a survey, more people would take the option to pray. We are raised to think that we operate under majority rule.

The only true value we should chase is our relationship with God, our families and those on whom we have an impact— the kids we teach or coach, our workers, our neighbors. We must stop strip mining others to meet our own needs, and discard people who have no more to give us when we discover a new toy or hobby or person who can better meet our needs.

As we became more prosperous, we paid for it at the expense of our relationships. We have more things and more money but enjoy them less and less. According to William Bennett, our society has come to place less value on what we owe others and on moral and social obligations and less on sacrifice as a moral good, less value on social conformity and respectability, and less value on restraint and modesty in matters of sexuality.

In future chapters, we will look at the stories behind these statistics. The people and their feelings, the trends and resources we have. To get back to where we need to be, we need discipline, good mentoring and love. We need home-grown heroes, the teachers and scout leaders. We need religion. This book will show how to begin to do just that!

**Chapter II**

# THE PROBLEM:
# WHAT CAUSES LIFE RAGE?

Rage is furious, uncontrolled anger, and in what we know as Life Rage, that anger can arise from the smallest of incidents, a minor issue that suddenly gains major importance and demands a major reaction. More to the point, it is usually based upon not just one incident but a series of them whereupon the impact builds up over time. One problem, sure, we can throw it off and ignore it—but when more problems begin to mount up, it's a very different story.

Let's look at a typical day in America and see how Life Rage works in action by watching it build up.

You get into the car and try to get on the freeway, where you have to fight for a break-in traffic because no one is going to give you one. There's a construction zone, but people are speeding through it, and some guy cuts you off just as you get to your exit, so you have to go down to the next one and backtrack, making you late for work. You chalk up some **road rage**.

You get to work, where no one has bothered to clean or refill the communal coffeepot and someone has taken your mug. An email tells you that Joe from the mailroom has been let go and has been making some threats about coming back, so there are new security procedures. You have tons of work, but the computer keeps going down, and your boss is saying nasty things about your job performance, even though you know you've done more than your share. Add a little **work rage**.

You go for lunch and stand in line for a burger, served by a sullen and rude counter girl, and on the way back to work you get to hear a call-in show about the latest jury verdict and why people are incensed about it and what they plan to do to the downtown that night. You switch over to a music station, but they are playing songs about taking it to the streets. And you yourself are not that happy about your latest tax assessment or that new initiative being proposed in Washington that the radio is now reporting. Call it **government rage**.

Go back to work, same stuff, different day, and then drive home through the same maddening rush-hour traffic. Stop at the bank and notice the chart at the door that tells the clerks just how tall any escaping robber might be. When you get home, your daughter is full of stories about how Billy is hitting other kids and calling them names, really, really bad names that she is not allowed to say. You know his parents have been called in but that they say it's the teacher's fault for picking on Billy, who only wants to express himself. Meanwhile, you are putting a compress on your son's eye where he got hurt, not in the baseball game, but in the fight afterward. You, and your children, now know what **school rage** is.

Your spouse arrives from a business trip, exhausted. He left Boston this morning for a two-hour flight home and just got in. The plane was delayed time after time and then it sat on the runway for an hour, with no attempts from the crew to let anyone know what was going on and no soft drinks served and no food, which is bad because your husband was afraid to leave the gate to grab a quick bite during the myriad of short delays for fear he'd miss the real departure. It finally took off, and here he is, cramped, hungry and a little worse for the wear. He has just brought in a load of **air rage**.

Finally, you eat dinner and sit down to pay the bills and watch a little television. You just can't figure out this health insurance—it makes no sense, and repeated calls to your insurer are met with busy signals, voice mails left, and no returned calls. What's on the tube? A true-to-life movie about a terrorist attack on agribusiness followed by a news report on riots against the nuclear plant. Finish your day with a dose of business rage.

If you lump them all together—work and school, road and air, government and business, you can just sum it up as **life rage**.

Life rage covers the gamut from petty incivilities like deliberately loud music from a passing car, one current favorite gibe among some young offenders, to an act as powerful and despicable as blowing up a government building in Oklahoma City. But ultimately, it is always irrational, because its outcome is not to make a situation better but to make it worse.

Take the kind of rage engendered by a typical day in America, and multiply it by the number of all the people in this country. Then multiply it by the number of days in the year, the day after unremitting day that it occurs. This is the accumulation of life rage. It is pervasive and unrelenting. We get it at work and at school, in the car and in the air, from our dealings with companies and with government. It means that the biggest threat to the safety and security of this country is not coming from a foreign nation or international terrorist organization but from disturbed, frustrated, hostile and angry neighbors and colleagues. As Pogo said, "We have met the enemy and he is us."

There are growing numbers of people who see normal settings such as schools, churches, offices and highways as places to act out their frustrations and gain personal satisfaction at whatever cost. Each of these will be dealt with in subsequent chapters, with the problem defined, causes given and some idea of solutions provided.

So what is fueling America's life rage? There are many causes.

## COMPETITIVENESS AND THE NEED TO ESTABLISH POWER

Winning isn't the most important thing—it's the only thing. In sports, in business, and even at school, we honor those who come in first. It's not enough to finish, we have to finish big. Coming in first, and being at the top give you some ascendancy over others.

Having that kind of power is good, because it means control. Much of rage is fueled by the need to control others with physical threats or with intimidation. If we can't control ourselves or our environment, we need to at least exert some control over others. After all, power isn't power until we can use it on other people.

But life rage happens when that power is thwarted, when you feel out of control. It is a scary thing to know that you have no control over events. And so, irrationally, you decide to seek some control and to assert some power over the situation, even though in the long run you will be damaging your own chances for any kind of good resolution to the problem. By trying to gain power over others, we lose it over ourselves and act not in our own best interests but from the stance of Life Rage.

Take driving, for example. In driving, competitiveness means that you have to beat out the other guy and to get there first, even if first only means being first at the next stop light, a mere twenty feet ahead of the next guy. With road rage, there truly can be no ties.

## MATERIALISM

Americans are buying more than they can afford. The size of our new single-family homes has grown in the past 40 years, from 1520 square feet in 1971 to 2195 square feet in 1998. So have our cars and our refrigerators. Family rooms and hot tubs are common, as are multiple bathrooms, a luxury in the 1990s.

In a *Detroit Free Press* poll, about 40% of respondents said they cannot afford everything they need for a comfortable life. We've added things like cell phones, DVD players, computers and personal assistants as a matter of course. And the cell phones, meant to be for emergencies, are used to ask what to buy for dinner or what video to pick up. Our kids demand not just stuff but precisely the right kind of stuff, with just the right label and with the right brand name. And lots of it.

Half of all Americans are going into debt to buy Christmas gifts, and 20% are still in debt the next Thanksgiving, yet many cannot even remember what gifts their spouses gave them the year before.

All of this consumption takes a toll in that we have to work to earn this stuff. Don Aslett, an author on cleaning up clutter, says that "too much" can often result in "too busy," not just in earning money to buy it but in cleaning it, maintaining it, insuring it, using it, talking about it. And then there is the ease of credit, which means the stress of seeing overdue bills come in and facing that increasingly common event, bankruptcy. A 1999 study at the National Institute for Personal Finance Employee Education found that 54% of workers worry about their debt, 34% rate financial stress from high to extreme, and 33% admit money worries hamper job performance.

Or if you don't want to work, you can count on winning the lottery, which used to be called the numbers racket. It is now run by the state and attracts customers with its own news show. We are a litigious society, where people think that a lawsuit is a kind of lottery, and if you win, you will be set up for life. We have more attorneys in this country than doctors, which means we are much more interested in getting even than getting well.

## SUBSTANCE ABUSE

Drugs and alcohol affect people of all ages, sexes and races, physical, ammonal and moral lives and they lead to legal, behavioral, emotional and financial problems. It is estimated that 73% of substance abusers are employed, according to the Institute for a Drug Free Workplace, and 5% to 17% of the workforce, depending on occupation, arrives at work under the influence of alcohol and/or drugs.

Addiction is everywhere, and it permeates the workplace, schools, and our homes. Society's infrastructure has been weakened by it, with societal changes that include a breakdown of values. Gang wars, prostitution, murder, drug trafficking and theft destroy neighborhoods, and moral standards are trivialized. It can lead to crime due to its ability to impede good decision-making and its economic demands for fulfillment. Drugs and alcohol, lead to kids being raised by grandparents or foster parents.

But there are parents who serve beer at teen parties and think it is perfectly okay to do so as the kids are going to drink anyway and they want to be on hand when the kids do drink. What this attitude tells is actually related to the next topic— lack of responsibility.

## LACK OF RESPONSIBILITY.

A used car salesman kidnapped a 30-year-old woman and held her hostage for over nine hours, raping her repeatedly. Was it his fault? No, according to his lawyer, who admittedly had an interest in the outcome. His client couldn't help himself; it was an "irresistible impulse" of which the perpetrator was also a victim.

In another case, the jury found a drunk driver guilty who had killed two people who were sitting in a car, but they recommended a reduced sentence because the defendant hadn't meant to do the deed and the victims hadn't suffered.

We've all heard by know of the Twinkie Defense that tried to get a city official off the hook for murder by blaming his sugar rush. It didn't work. But what did is the prosecution that got McDonald's blamed for the fact that a woman was burned when she spilled hot coffee on herself.

Smokers now blame the cigarette companies for their emphysema, pregnant girls blame the school for not teaching better, and the government is responsible for keeping drug addicts healthy by providing clean needles.

But what about the man with active AIDS who participates in unprotected sex and refuses to tell his partners of his status, putting their lives at risk? It's another example of that all-powerful word, attitude, wherein self-centeredness and self-importance are considered not only the norm but stances to be admired and emulated. It's not rare: Two-thirds of gay men in Chicago, Denver and San Francisco said they had unprotected sex at least once in an 18-month period, and 30% of young gay men in seven other cites reported having unprotected sex, 7% of them HIV positive.

Parents are too often deadbeat dads with no idea of responsibility for the children they create. I've had real cases like a client by the name of Pam, who lost $800,000 in child support from a deadbeat ex-husband who was nowhere to be found. For 14 years, he avoided paying child support as she struggled to pay medical fees for two physically challenged children. When I tracked him down, I found out the man not only had a good business, but had warmed up to several rich women and their families in three countries. Living high on the hog in Cleveland, Ohio, he claimed to be suffering from a vindictive wife.

## TECHNOLOGY AND CHANGE

This was best described in Alvin Toffler's *Future Shock*, where he described the fleeting nature of technological change and how it affects societal change. The stress of dealing with change, he said, can make one ill with *Future Shock*, and always shifting social norms can lead to unclear expectations and anomie. With that, the increasing amount of choice in the world.

For instance, you used to have one phone, which was black, and one phone bill. You knew how to use the phone with no training—it was instinctive. Now making a call can involve a choice of using one of the land-lines, with their options like three-way calling and call waiting, or the cell phone, which you are trying to use after hours and weekends to reduce your long-distance payments. And you have an answering machine to check, as well as voice mail, and you could check the cell phone messages if you only knew how to retrieve them.

There are seemingly hundreds of plans and programs to choose from when it comes to accessing and paying for all of this. One phone bill from one phone company that everyone uses becomes three bills, one in the mail for local service that you pay with a check, one online that just takes the money out of your account, and another one for all the cell calls. Whew. Toffler points out that such choices can be overwhelming, causing worry and frustration.

Social change results from technological change, as always. Someone from a few generations ago would see our computers and ATMs and SUVs, but they would be most appalled at the incredible number of young unmarried girls having babies with no means of support and pornographer Larry Flynt using the First Amendment so handily in bringing down the Speaker of the House, to the applause of millions.

With all this technological change comes fast living and stress. We can get more things done faster, so we do. We can be hooked up to the rest of the world, so we are. There is a rapid changing of jobs, an aging workforce, and almost constant mergers. Computers and other technologies have given us a chance to do more and more work and to let our employers keep closer tabs on us and on our productivity. Job hopping is happening more than ever in the past, with a resultant lack of a knowledgeable workforce. Other pervasive changes include changing homes more often, and even changing spouses. Indeed, change of this nature—rapid change—keeps us off balance, destroys our sense of security and leads to the ruination of relationships and a sense of community.

It works within the family too. American families, and their kids, seem to be always on the move. Kids are at sports and camps and play dates and lessons and they have to be driven to all these places. They are scheduled to a fare-thee-well. Sports events are all too often held on holidays, so the family outing is sacrificed to junior's hockey game. Or even a practice. Even Christmas Day.

Fit all that in with mom and dad's jobs and a vacation and the needs of life like shopping and there is little time to sit around and think and play and dream. And because of this, old-fashioned family activities like board games, where people sit around and talk after dinner, are going out of style in favor of electronic handhelds that people play alone. Critics since Alexis de Tocqueville have found that we are a hyperactive nation.

But when a company in Dallas, Siemens, actually conducted a contest to find the busiest family, they found, contrary to what you may think, that these families were thoughtful about what they were doing and had devised meaningful activities for themselves meant to help cure old problems of grief and loneliness.

## ECONOMICS

Related to this idea of living at hyperspeed is our changing economy that is still turning from a manufacturing base to a knowledge based one while at the same time moving to globalization. New technologies have reduced the need to hire younger workers, as they have given us added productivity that reduces the need for the unskilled and semi-skilled while boosting the need for skilled workers. However, as older workers retire, there will be no one to take their places.

Management guru Peter Drucker calls this demographic fact the dominant factor in business in the next two decades. As underdeveloped countries gain in population, the developed industrial nations will lose it, giving these countries an edge.

The worker dearth in the western countries means a shift to less labor-intensive products and services, the substitution of capital and technology for labor, or outsourcing to third world countries.

But what this means for the average worker is change—constant change—as industries move and grow and shrink, and as companies do as well. It is said that people now expect to stay on the job for only a year, or they are hired for work on the basis of what project is available. This may seem to be exciting news for some, but it carries with it the need to be constantly proving oneself for the new boss, because there is always a boss. A stream of new jobs is in a way like a serial marriage, where you constantly have to forge new relationships and develop new ways of working as a team. And sometimes, productivity has to wait while the learning curve resolves itself and a new workflow is formed. Constant reinvention of how to do things takes a toll on resources.

In addition, this work style takes a toll on family life. Longer hours and more stress mean less time with spouse and kids and parents. It is a constant complaint today, and many polls have shown that workers, offered a choice between more money and more time off, would choose the latter. Problems with the workforce today have led to another big problem, solitude.

## SOLITARINESS AND ALIENATION

We are now a nation of the unattended. Kids are left home alone and the house burns down. Babies are left to die in unattended cars in the summertime. Or three kids are left in a running car that slips out of gear and runs into a wooden landscaping timber. A stepfather stands idly by while his 16-year-old jumps from the roof onto a burning table to emulate a professional wrestling match. A kid says that he'd rather "be wanted for murder than not wanted at all."

Kids sit around all day and listen to music and watch TV and videos, learning a whole lot about violence and sex. But they are not learning how to deal with others from adult mentors or taught any of the social skills, much less how to read and write, and there is no other intervening factor or activity in their young lives.

Kids are left alone especially after school, in the danger hours between 3:00 and 7:00 P.M., when most crimes by children are committed because of opportunity. And instead of a nuclear family, they have virtual families, be they actors on the soap operas or Internet companions who could be almost anyone. They turn to their peers instead of to the nuclear families. And the rise of unmarried mothers having kids has led to what has been called fatherless-son syndrome, leading children to turn to youth gangs as a way to feel like they belong and to give them a sense of rules and structure that they long for.

Fatherless boys, whether they are children of single moms, divorced mothers or widows, are, in overall, more than twice as likely to go to jail, even if all other things such as family income or the mother's educational level are the same. It is the absence of time with dad that seems to be the factor. Income and the fact that the mother had been married to the father did make a difference, but the presence of a stepfather was found to be a detriment. But even if the fathers are there, the kids' fathers and the kids' mothers are way too often letting the kids stay up late, not helping them with homework and not going to teacher conferences or PTA meetings.

## DOMESTIC VIOLENCE

Another actual case I was personally involved in was with a lady by the name of Lisa. Lisa's ex-husband attempted to kill her and their daughter by driving his vehicle directly head on into her vehicle shortly after she picked up the child from their public neutral meeting spot. The divorce had just been finalized. Both wife and daughter were taken to the hospital, and the ex-husband fled on foot and was captured three days later. He got only three years in prison, but his letters and pagers from there were ablaze with death threats. A sympathetic ex-cop helped procure a new identity for Lisa and her daughter, at no charge, and I am providing some security as well, so there will be one less woman victimized by an enraged man. Meanwhile, she loses so much, including her ties to the past and family solidarity.

Because of all of these things, the nature of violence in America is changing; it is now more common for the young and mentally disturbed to commit crimes and engage in acts of violence than at any other time in history. And because the victims of any crime are most likely to be similar to the perpetrators, in many cases, the victims are also children. The reverberations of this are felt everywhere: lost innocence, a cynical and apathetic view toward society, kids with post-traumatic stress disorder, and pervasive fear.

So they have created gangs and trench coat mafias and disaffected Goth groups with their own way of dressing and acting and position themselves as outcasts, mad loners and deeply original thinkers, even though there is an entire bunch of kids behind them dressed the same and acting the same.

It all relates to the 60s, which ushered in an era when we were to question authority on a knee-jerk basis, and disobedience of rules was considered the norm. Never mind what the rules said or how sensible they were. We were not to be constrained. Coloring outside the lines was the only way to go. So, a generation of kids never learned that the lines were there to teach skills—fine motor skills. Art itself is no longer meant to show hard-won skill or technique but to express the artist's angst at the state of the world he finds himself in. So, the art that is touted and given grants and defended consists of a crucifix in urine, a photo of a whip handle protruding from someone's rectum, or a man sprinkling the crowd with his own HIV-positive blood.

Edginess is cool, and angst is popular, and if you see a bunch of teens or musicians or whatever featured in the Sunday supplement, they will be sure to be caught scowling at the camera and maybe making gang signs to show how little they care of what you think.

Adults are affected as well by loneliness. The sense of community is suffering as more and more people affect a solitary lifestyle. There has even been a book written about it. The book, *Bowling Alone*, decries today's lack of a civic foundation to life. And a civic life and civil behavior are closely related.

## XENOPHOBIA

The most common fear in the world, it is said, but one we do not deal with, is the fear of the stranger. In fact, the growth of diversity in today's America is now being touted as the American dilemma, or one of them.

Horrifying hate crimes are often in the news, fueled by racism, religious intolerance, homophobia, and immigration. The images conjured up by names such as James Byrd, Jr., the Jasper, Texas, man dragged by a white gang behind a truck until he was dismembered, or Matthew Shepard, a gay student in Laramie, Wyoming, who was beaten, tied to a fence and left for dead in Wyoming. A light-skinned black man is killed in a bar because black patrons thought he was white and did not want his kind drinking there.

There is discord to be found both in the fear of those unlike ourselves, and our perceived need to compete with them to hold our own turf, and in the anger that the other groups we despise are creating overall changes in the American culture.

This generates a tremendous amount of frustration. The Intelligence Project saw a rise in the number of hate groups from 474 in 1997 to 537 in 1998, and there has also been a rise in the number of hate group Web sites, which grew by 60%. And they are not always known by their swastikas or their Klan hoods. Some can mask themselves behind the most seemingly innocuous fronts, such as a religious, cultural or patriotic group, and be embraced by politicians, academics and civic leaders.

All of these social and economic conditions could make a person paranoid. Is there any hope? Yes, indeed, there is. There is always, first of all, a personal choice in how we conduct our own lives and how we raise our children. And there is the fact that we can work with others to change things.

Each of the next few chapters in this book will cover one of the six major rages: school rage, work rage, road rage, air rage, anti-government rage and anti-business rages. There will be some scary statistics and some horrifying anecdotes. There will be an analysis of how and why these things have come to be. And then there will be a listing of ways that you can work against these forces in your own life and some hopeful ideas about ways that others have found to ameliorate the six rages we call life rage.

The opposite of rage is calmness, peace, and control. By attending to our own self and family life and by working together with others in our communities and through our government and businesses, we can attain life peace and help to create it in the world around us.

**Chapter III**

# School Rage: The Problem and Its Causes

When you think of schools, what used to come to mind? Erasers, blackboards, lockers and band camp? Clean-cut young athletes, scholars carrying books, angelic-looking kids in choir robes?

Schools are supposed to be places of peace where new ideas should flourish. Today, however, the new thoughts include sending the kids off to schools that could turn into news like the ones in Littleton, Colorado, or Jonesboro, Arkansas, or Paducah. Kentucky, or Conyers, Georgia.

Parents getting the kids ready for school could be thinking of Nathaniel Brazill, a 13-year-old in West Palm Beach who shot his teacher because the man wouldn't let the kid, in detention for throwing water balloons, go talk to two girls.

Or of Kip Kinkel, a 16-year-old who, in Springfield, Oregon, in 1998, propped the door to the cafeteria open with his foot and opened fire. When the carnage was over, he had killed two classmates, one in cold blood at short range by shooting the back of his head as he lay under a table trying to hide. He had also killed his parents and wounded 15 other students.

In his journal, read aloud for the first time at the trial, Kinkel revealed a level and intensity of rage that has become frighteningly familiar because of other killings in schools across the country. "I am so full of rage . . . Blowing the school up or walking into a pep assembly with guns . . . that is how I will repay all you . . . They won't laugh after they are scraping pieces of their parents, sisters, brothers, and friends from my wall of hate."

Because of the horror of too many names of schools and towns in shock, students and parents in the United States feel that kids spend their days under the threat of violence and crime. In a study conducted by the U.S. Department of Education's National Center for Employment Statistics, approximately 11% of U.S. twelfth-graders said they had been threatened in school during the month prior to the study, while internationally, only 7% on average reported having been threatened at school.

The Department of Justice and Education produced a report in 1998 to inform educators, parents and students about the current nature of crime in U.S. schools. Their findings are disheartening . . . and horrifying. Far from being safe and secure for students, teachers and staff, our schools too often are the scene of mayhem and murder. Another government entity, the Center for Disease Control's National Center for Injury Prevention found in a 1999 study that multiple-student injuries caused by school violence rose from 1996 to 1999.

In addition to the mayhem reported above, there are other horror stories of problems that were averted, the names you didn't hear. Five teenage boys in Burlington, Wisconsin were arrested when a classroom-to-classroom bloodbath they were planning came unraveled. The boys allegedly planned to seek revenge on teachers, students and administrators at Burlington High School who had picked on them. The boys, often dressed in black, listened to heavy-metal music and liked classmates to think they worshipped Satan.

In Jackson Township, Ohio, a 14-year-old boy admitted to police that he had a "hit list" of classmates he'd like to kill.

Police say the youth had access to a firearm and allegedly had stated that he was going to take it to school and use it.

Because of worrisome reports such as these, drug-sniffing dogs, metal detectors, armed guards in the halls, and violent kids are all now part of the new American education scene. The National School Boards Association decries the "epidemic of violence" in our schools—evidenced by the fact that 82% of 729 school districts responding to a recent association survey said that violence in their schools has increased in the last five years, with no end to that escalation in sight.

A Metropolitan Life study said that more than 10% of teachers and nearly one quarter of all students had been victims of violence in or near their schools. And that violence, as we have learned to our sorrow, is not confined to urban schools, but is on the rise in rural and suburban schools as well.

There were 255,000 non-fatal serious violent crimes, in which students aged 12-18 were the victims, which occurred in our schools in 1996 alone. That same year, 5% of 12th graders reported that they had been injured with a weapon during the previous 12 months, either at school or on the school bus. At the middle and high school levels, physical attack or violence without a weapon was the most commonly reported crime.

It gets worse. Teachers were victims of 1,581,000 nonfatal crimes at schools over a five-year period (1992-1996). Nathaniel Brazill is a case in point. From 1992 through 1994, 76 kids were murdered or committed suicide at school—an ever-increasing statistic today. These statistics affect everyone, although we prefer to think, "It can't happen to our kids." But all too often, it can—and does.

But not in the inner city. With all the emphasis on school shootings, it is important to remember one population that seems—so far—not to be affected by mass shootings and random massacres, the inner city school. There is certainly a problem here with kids killing kids, but it does not take place in the school setting. It is usually a neighborhood problem caused by non-students, and schools are not defensible turf.

Several reasons have been given for this. Existing tight security in schools, with guards and metal detector gates. Existing programs for conflict resolution. A gang structure that targets its victims as equal competitors and moves violence to a more "professional" sphere. Guns seen automatically as big trouble rather than non-threatening and normal hunting implement. A cramped setting where it's harder to move in weaponry and to escape after violence.

Of course, if one were to add up the violence in the inner city that occurs on a case-by-case basis and lump it into one event that could have happened in school, it would draw as much attention as Columbine or Joplin. And no matter if the violence occurs in the classroom or in the street, it still affects our kids, and we must find the causes and deal with them.

## WHAT'S CAUSING THIS?

The causes of school rage are many and are interconnected. A big part of the problem is that schools are no longer places to learn academics, reading, writing and arithmetic. Now, schools have been asked to teach nutrition, health, vocational education, safety, driving, and sex education. They must also provide breakfasts and lunches, teach in all languages to all kinds of students of all levels of ability and to solve social inadequacies from teen parenting to character education. And all of this in 180 days a year, versus 220 eight-hour days in Japan and 240 6.5-hour days in Europe. In 1950, American students had a longer time in the classroom than Japanese students.

Also a factor is the fact that public schools are forced to work with students with all levels of preparation and interest in education. Unlike widget makers, they cannot ship back faulty resources but instead must make do with them and try to optimize them.

However, when we try to get more specific about the problem, one of the biggest reasons for today's school troubles is seen in the sad cries of the messages that Kinkel and others leave behind as their legacies. And that is bullying.

## BULLYING

Bullying is now seen in a new light; that puts a new interpretation on the schoolyard bullies of our youth. Not just a simple "nyah, nyah, nyah" or "you have cooties" interchange, it is repeated and aggressive systematic behavior that deliberately causes physical or psychological intimidation and torment. It can take the form of taunting and name-calling, intimidation and psychological aggression, as well as vandalism of personal property, and even gestures.

It is often based on a rigid social system of in and out groups, cliques and lonely loners, where a clique forms and picks on others. Examples are myriad. Josh Sneed, a slight freshman in Powell, Tennessee, who tried to fight back against a group of skateboarders called the Skaters who threatened him with chains and bats, ended up with four titanium plates in his skull. He was rescued by a football player but has to learn how to walk and talk again.

Unfortunately, there are kids in every part of the country who can understand the fear, hopelessness and rage he felt. Some become victims of themselves. Sophomore Brian Head of Etowah High in Georgia was so distraught from being bullied that he killed himself in front of an economics class. No one was held responsible for driving him to his death.

Others who are bullied have been known to turn around and visit their frustration on someone even weaker and lower on the social scale than they are, so, bullying can be both endured and committed by the perpetrators of the crimes.

But many strike back and turn on their oppressors, or the world in general. Sixteen-year-old Evan Ramsey, an outcast at Bethel Regional High in Bethel, Alaska, got tired of being spit on and beat up. He tried fighting back, ineptly, and reporting the problems to the principal, who got tired of dealing with it.

Punishing the bullies did no good. He got even by shooting into the air or randomly at passersby, and eventually killed his principal and another student. "I felt a sense of power with a gun," he said from his jail cell. "It was the only way to get rid of the anger."

And there is Andy Williams, a 15-year-old in Santana High in Santee, California, who shot 15 and killed two in response to constant verbal torment and abuse. Or Elizabeth Bush, an eighth grader from Williamsport, Pennsylvania, who shot one of her few friends because the friend, to fit in, had betrayed her and joined in with a group of taunters.

A 2000 report by the Secret Service found that in two-thirds of the 37 school shootings, the shooters reported feeling "persecuted, bullied, threatened, attacked or injured." William Pollack, a psychologist and author who contributed to the study, said that Columbine students told him bullying was rampant at the school; it was the norm.

The National Education Association says that 160,000 kids skip school every day because they are intimidated by their classmates, and a National Institutes of Health study published in 2001 shows that almost a third of those from ages 11 to 15, 5.7 million across the country have been bullied. That is a lot of pain and anger and a lot of lost opportunity to do what the kids should be doing—learning.

Why do kids bully? This is a culture that values strength, control and power, and especially power over others. In sports, in corporations, in the media, we reward winners. Bullies are defined as children who take repeated hostile actions against another child and who have more power than those they target. Bullies have learned the lesson of the importance of power, at least, and they are aggressive not in response to a situation but rather regardless of circumstances. They commit their crimes serially, and they are increasing in number. These dangerous individuals are usually introverted, intelligent, and hard to detect. And because bullying can be very subtle, teachers and others too often do not work to resolve these problems, and those in charge may not realize the seriousness of the problem until it is too late. Bullies can be glib about their actions and do not accept responsibility for them, according to clinical psychologist William Porter. Porter is the co-author of a book on reducing bullying in schools.

Bullies, he says, want attention. In agreement is David Miller, an assistant professor of social work at Case Western Reserve University in Cleveland. Kids shoot because shooting gets attention, he says, and because our society is addicted to violence.

Another problem is the parent who only wants a child who is a winner. For instance, there is the story of "Smoking Joe"— the kid I talked about in the first chapter.

## CRAVING FOR ATTENTION

Unfortunately, the need for attention creates another cause for school shootings, as in the case of the imitator. The copycat. Competitiveness in American society rears its ugly head even here, as unbalanced teens try to outdo each other in angst and in response to it. This angst, disconnection and disenfranchisement are often seen in a subculture of youth that plays up its alienation from society and families and makes a game of it, be it with Goth clothes and sensibilities or a skinhead orientation.

It is said that loneliness is the primary problem that plagues adolescents. Kids report feeling increasingly alone, ignored and alienated, unable to connect to the rest of society and with no moral guidance. Bereft of this, they enter into a peer culture to get the sense of acceptance and belongingness they need from cliques. Or they create an alternative identity, say as a computer game geek, Goth or skinhead, that will give them a world in which they can live in with rules they can understand and a tribe where they can fit in and get attention.

Unfortunately, the worlds they create may be based on casual violence, power tripping or meanness, and kids will do almost anything to get the attention they crave and the respect this mini-society offers them. In their world, they can live by their own *Lord of the Flies* rulebook.

In the face of this, society seems to have abdicated its role in bringing the kids to heel when they go too far, with an "anything goes" mentality that will prove how hip we all are. Though adolescence is when kids need to break from their families and establish their own identities, they are apparently doing this now with no help from adults and with complete acceptance for whatever they want to do. Columbine's Harris and Klebold made a murderous video for a class, and no one remarked it or seemed to point out it might not be such a good idea.

## VIOLENCE IN SOCIETY

Also potentially at fault are movies, music and computer and video games that glorify violence and either train kids on how to do it well or at least desensitize them to it.

The American Psychological Association finds the evidence that lines media violence to teen violence overwhelming and says that "to argue against it is to argue against gravity," while Ted Turner calls TV violence the single most significant factor contributing to American violence. A 1995 study by the American Academy of Pediatrics says media violence is the single most remediable factor of all causes of violent crime in the U.S., and CBS President Leslie Moonves says that "anyone who thinks the media has nothing to do with [the Columbine shootings] is an idiot."

Meanwhile, the Department of Education says that kids watch TV for 1640 hours a year, vs. 1000 in school, and 52% have TVs in their bedrooms. Preschoolers see nearly 10,000 violent episodes yearly, and by the age of 12, kids have seen 50,000 killings and hundreds of thousands of other violent acts.

The public health community agrees that 30 years of research show that entertainment violence leads to increases in aggressive attitudes, values and behavior, especially in kids, and that video games are the most severe stimuli of all TV shows, music and movies.

But kids sit with joysticks in their hands and work to shoot down the other guy, and not necessarily a bad guy like a Nazi in a World War II simulation game but just another guy like you, with extra points for getting blood to spurt the farthest, all accompanied by actual cries of pain and anguish. Fun, no?

The debate goes on about the violence training that potentially exists from video games. I believe the debate is over—the school shootings in Paducah, Kentucky, have shown clearly that certain video games train our youth to be killers, to enjoy violence and to become desensitized to many gruesome acts of violence. The shooter at Paducah, Kentucky, Michael Carneal, had no previous firearms training except for his extensive training on violent video games. He fired eight shots at a student group and accomplished eight hits on eight different students, five head shots and three upper torso, leaving three dead and one paralyzed. His hit-the-target ratio was significantly higher than police officers with extensive training.

Where did he get his training? He is an avid and addicted video game user. Where did he instinctively shoot for? The head and torso deadly areas. Why didn't the screaming and pleading affect him? He hears it all the time during video game shootings. You be the judge.

Kids listen to lyrics like, "Kill the bitches," where rappers brag about raping and murdering their mothers. It's true that there was music about death and murder in the old days, but in songs like "Tom Dooley," "Stagger Lee" or "Frankie and Johnny," the violence was seen as a negative thing that took a human toll. Crime and violence generally had consequences, or it was at least presented as something that was not such a great idea, and that view was supported by society as a whole. Now, however, not only do kids listen to the most outrageous lyrics, with first-person advocacy of some of the most appalling violence against those near and dear, but societal analysts chime in about the authenticity and power of the work. People like Paul McCartney and even Pat Boone praise the attitude of Eminem's lyrics, and mainstream columnists hoped that the Grammy Awards wouldn't "cop out" by not presenting him with the award.

Another change has been in the pervasiveness and ubiquity of violence. Many kids see violent images—whether in the movies or on the news, whether in a natural disaster or a man-made one—and they are not affected. But when the images of violence become the norm and occur over and over with increasing regularity, on news coverage that goes on 24/7, it tends to overwhelm some of the more fragile kids.

Today's pervasiveness does not let them put the problem into a perspective where the violence is just one of a number of events in life. There are many vulnerable children who are overwhelmed, who have experienced a family problem, or who feel like misfits, and these need special attention before they become aggressors themselves. They must not learn to be insensitive to violence or to grow up thinking that violence is a way to solve problems.

# GUNS

Kids also do this with guns. Too often, when bullied kids have nowhere to turn, they turn to the obvious remedy for their problems—guns, the great equalizer between bully and victim. Kids carry weapons to school, both to protect themselves and to use in the commission of crimes. They are the victims of—or the perpetrators of—crimes of every description, from assault and arson, to rape and murder.

You can't have a school shooting without one, after all, and there is a prevalence of guns in our country. In one recent year, for example, firearms killed no children in Japan, 19 in Great Britain, 57 in Germany, 109 in France, 153 in Canada—and 5,285 in the U.S. And for every child killed by a gun, four are wounded. The rate of firearm deaths of children through age 14 is almost 12 times higher here than in the 25 other industrialized countries combined. Firearms kill 10 times more people than polio does.

The two 17-year-olds at Columbine had amassed two shotguns, an assault rifle, and an assault pistol that they used to shoot 26 kids and a teacher and kill 13 people before turning their armament on themselves.

It's no secret that today's teenagers are far more likely to engage in risky behavior like gun-toting than did kids in years past. Study after study blasts us with the statistics: The leading causes of death for teenagers (in order) are: accidents and crashes involving alcohol, homicide, and suicide. The later two are far too often the result of having guns easily available. In 1996, more than 1,300 kids from 10 to 19 years of age committed suicide with firearms. Two thirds of successful teen suicides involve a gun.

Of course, not all the guns and gun-related killings occur in the schools, but in 1996-7, over 6,000 students were expelled for bringing guns to school. It is estimated by the Journal of the American Medical Association that between 36% and 50% of male eleventh graders thought they could easily get a gun if they wanted one. The two kids at Columbine did, buying a pistol and 100 bullets from a 22-year-old man the night before they went on their rampage. That man faces 18 years in prison. All four of the weapons used in Littleton were gotten from unlicensed dealers at gun shows, and 10% of the guns used in crimes by juveniles and kids were sold at gun shows and flea markets.

It's important to remember that guns by themselves are not the problem. In Switzerland, shooting matches are public events, which mean people walk around with firearms, 13-year-olds keep score, and 16-year-olds compete as equals, while 12-to-14-year-olds have their own contests. Yet the country has a very low rate of gun-related violence, and many crimes involving firearms are committed by tourists. The widespread ownership of guns and its militia heritage is one reason Hitler did not invade the country, it is said. The reason for Swiss peacefulness? Attorney and author Stephen Halbrook attributes it to the country's sense of civic virtue, the attitude in which the firearm is held.

It was commonplace for Boy Scouts, 4-H-ers, and even some schools to hold shooting competitions and riflery exhibitions. It is not the guns themselves, I reiterate, that are the problem, but the culture that surrounds the guns and our attitudes toward them. There is a need for smart handling of guns, especially in the homes, and the need for the improved manufacture of guns, with better safety mechanisms, trigger locks, a harder trigger pull resistance, and load indicators. These things are similar to seat belts and door locks that keep kids from falling out of cars.

## DRUGS

When it comes to drugs, parents need to have their eyes opened. Drugs are present in children's lives, even though Mom and Dad pretend it isn't so. Statistics from a recent study reveal that 36% of parents surveyed believe their children has taken a drink, while actually 66% of students had done so. In the same study, 14% of parents thought their kids had tried cigarettes, while the number of students who reported that they had smoked was 41%. While only 5% of parents thought their kids have ever used illicit drugs, the actual figure was 17%.

In another study, in 1998, just about 10% of youth aged 12 to 17 said they used illegal drugs, from marijuana to crack, to inhalants, according to a National Household Survey. What's worse, an estimated 1.1 million of kids that year met the diagnostic criteria for dependence on these drugs. They became abusers, not just users.

A report by the National Center on Addiction and Substance Abuse at Columbia University says that drugs are used and sold in 60% of high schools and 30% of middle schools, involving 14 million students. It goes on to say that this is due to malignant neglect by parents, educators, students and the community. It criticizes the idea that kids can safely try drugs or alcohol without having problems with them, and it says schools spent $41 billion on substance abuse and addiction in 2001.

One problem with drugs is that like Hydra, it keeps growing new heads. Today, schools do not just need to deal with the classic drugs but also with new ones like ecstasy, designer drugs and even date rape drugs such as roofies. Ecstasy seems tailor-made for the young. It is energizing and slightly hallucinogenic. It is geared to a partying crowd. It suppresses the appetite. It is seen as harmless. It makes sex better.

It is also a consumer item, marketed like tennis shoes or makeup with logos and everything. It is praised on the Internet as a way to achieve fulfillment and insight. It is cheap, and therefore profitable. And it is rising in use, with confiscations on the increase by a whopping 450% between 1998 and 1999, with that number predicted to soar in the years after. Also on the rise: the number of emergency room admissions it causes.

## THE AGONY OF ECSTASY

Parents worried about "date rape" drugs and new designer drugs like "ecstasy" have another worry—these drugs can now be concocted in any average neighborhood. Methamphetamines can be made in the kitchen sink, with ammonia and other over-the-counter ingredients. The highly explosive mixtures are a concern for property owners. The latest synthetic drug crops are stronger today than they've ever been.

I predict a dramatic increase in the synthetic drugs trend. There's no importation involved, no smuggling necessary. Simply produce it when and where you want and in the quantity you'd like. Synthetic drugs answer the cry of bigger, better, quicker highs. Addiction time is faster, which means increased traffic and higher profit for the dealer. Parents and users beware: At any time, any drugs can shut the body down and you're dead.

Unfortunately, drug use and violence are connected and indeed interdependent on each other. In a 1995 survey, the School Crime Supplement to the National Crime Victimization Survey, it was found that schools with drug problems were more likely to suffer from violence. Kids with drugs, it was found, were also likely to have experienced violence, and those who said they knew of drug deals at school were also more likely to report that they were the subjects of physical attack, robbery and bullying. In turn, school gun violence was seen to be linked to drugs, with gang or drug disputes cited as the leading cause of drug school violence.

Teen marijuana use was also linked to violence, with frequent users from 12 to 17 four times more likely to attack others physically than kids who did not do drugs, according to the National Household Survey. And even if drug use is down, as has been seen since this survey was taken, the linkages between drugs and violence are still there.

## GANGS

They may be getting their drugs from a local gang member. Gangs are groups of kids, usually male but increasingly female, who engage in aggressive and delinquent acts within the gang and outside it as they fight other gangs. They are increasingly involved in drug trafficking, intimidation and violence.

It is estimated that urban youths will join gangs about 15% to 30% of the time, according to the Department of Justice. Studies show that gangs are responsible for 68% to 89% of all juvenile violent offenses, depending on the city. What's more, the influence of the gang is long lasting, with former members continuing to commit crimes.

Gangs are one way adolescents have in achieving a family

to bond with to obtain a sense of identity, protection, and a structured lifestyle.

## DEPRESSION

Much that we have discussed above—bullying, lack of family closeness, the rapid pace of life, low self-esteem—contribute to mental illness in teenagers and the possibility that anger and violence will be turned against the self. Depression affects many children, and a 1999 survey said that 20% of high schoolers have seriously considered suicide, and 8 to 11 of every 100,000 teens actually follow through. Indeed, many school shooters and gang members are motivated to commit suicide by police. Depression is called the most common emotional problem in adolescents, and it causes a host of family and school problems.

New tests allow us to screen kids for depression, and mental health campaigns are raising awareness of the problem, just as new therapies and studies are finding ways to help cure the disease. Meanwhile, parents should listen to kids, have them screened and get help from professionals if needed. Beyond that, parents should lock up guns and medications and make sure teens know the dangers they face as being especially vulnerable to drugs and drinking.

## SPORTS

Many of the bullies who have created America's love for power and control have been emulating America's current icons: athletes. Extreme competitors and superstars are the people our children admire, perhaps right next to rock stars and rappers. Sometimes these superstars are moral, hardworking leaders, like Michael Jordan. But sometimes they are ... well ... more like Dennis Rodman. And jocks who are admired are often not admired for their skill on the field, but for less desirable attributes.

A few years ago, an athletic product sponsor decided to use Rodman in its holiday season commercial. In the commercial, a conversation takes place between Rodman and Santa Claus. Rodman, with hair dyed white and nose ring intact, walks into a department store and tells Santa that he wants some new shoes. Santa points out to Rodman that he led the NBA in personal fouls, and there is a clip of Rodman punching someone. Next, Santa reminds Rodman of how he didn't follow the rules, skipped practices, and how he was suspended. Then Rodman says, "But I led the league in rebounds." So Santa looks at the elf at his side and says, "OK—give him the shoes." Does this attempt at "humor" teach kids that it doesn't matter if you're good or bad? That it doesn't matter how you win as long as you win?

Too many athletes in all sports and at all levels are losing any pretence at being role models as they rape, chat, fight and use drugs yet suffer few or no consequences and are honored and emulated by millions. They may be paid way beyond what their performance indicates solely due to their popularity.

Unfortunately, some of the drugs these athletes are using at the high school level are anabolic steroids. And because physicians rarely prescribe steroids for athletic use, most steroids used illegally are gotten on the black market. The National Institute of Drug Abuse estimates steroid sales on the black market at $400 million a year. They have some major side effects, such as withered testicles, sterility and impotence in males and irreversible masculinization in females. Some side effects, such as heart attacks and strokes, may not show up until years later. The destruction of talented bodies and disciplined minds through the use of steroids is a commonplace tragedy among our young athletes.

However, one side effect of steroids deserves special mention when we consider the topic of this book, and that is "roid rage." The psychological effects of steroids in both sexes include aggressive, combative behavior, as well as depression. How much of today's school rage is the result of athletes' relying too much on these drugs for mastery of their bodies instead of training and discipline?

Today, at least 40 million American youth participate in

organization sports in addition to sports at school and kids are no longer just doing it for fun or to keep busy after school. They are pressured to meet professional standards, to win championships or scholarships and to be ultra competitive, no matter what the cost is. For boys, it's important to play, part of the male psyche and identity.

It is not surprising that some of this extreme love of competitiveness and physical strength carries over into everyday school life. Jocks are feted and rewarded, held unaccountable for behavior and grades, and not reined in when they take their game face behavior and physical advantages of the playing field and out of the gym and into the classroom and hallways.

Unfortunately, we see these mean-spirited actions reflected at youth games as well. Kids deliberately hit, spike or kick each other. One young athlete just got into trouble for breaking the jaw of another—on purpose. And even dodge ball is now coming under attack on the playground for being too violent.

And it's not just violence by the participants but also by the parents in something that is being called sideline sport rage:

- In Boston, the father of one hockey player was beaten to death by the father of another.
- The father of a Pony League football player was arrested for assaulting a referee who claimed the boy caught the ball out of bounds.
- In Repton, Alaska, military police were called to stop a parents' brawl at a kid's football game.

But sports leaders are striking back in an attempt to teach kids the true value of sports and sportsmanship. Recently, in Ohio, after being disgusted with heckling parents, one soccer coach and his team agreed to try a silent game; no parents were allowed to cheer, to vocalize any opinions or say anything at all to the players or the coach. A youth sports league in West Palm Beach, Florida, recently began requiring all parents of those wishing to play or cheer for its soccer team to take an ethics class, becoming the first group in the nation to require sportsmanship training for parents as a prerequisite. And the American Youth Soccer Organization is extending nationally a pilot program called Kids' Zone designed to stamp out sideline violence by asking parents to sign pledges that they will not disrupt games.

Unfortunately, we continue to coach, with winning as our main goal. I hope that someday we adjust our coaching attitude to match our youth's desire . . . to have fun and participate in sports with their friends. Additionally, youth sports participation is one of the "Building Blocks" to our future generation's self-esteem, character, respect, work ethics and numerous other skills that our country so desperately need, especially in the workplace.

Indeed, many of the ills being suffered by the youth of America can be laid at their parents' doors, but some of this results are not from too much parental involvement in the kids' lives, but from too little. Work has become the center of many families in the U.S. Parents are so busy earning a living that they don't have adequate time to spend with their children. This is true not only in families who must work long hours to make ends meet but in more affluent ones as well. Some parents work only to provide their children with luxuries and to provide themselves with every material possession.

Unfortunately, far too many parents do not see certain behaviors such as bullying and name calling, fighting and acting up in class, as unacceptable. Many say that they themselves behaved this way, and they provide no discipline at home, so teachers spend the school day instilling it in the classroom rather than teaching. Parents let their kids stay up until wee hours. They do not help their kids with homework or demand that it be done, and they indiscriminately back the child over the teacher and encourage disrespect. They do not care about education and do not show up at school-related activities or teacher conferences. There are second graders in regular classes in Detroit who do not know how old they are, or when their own birthdays are. Obviously, the parents are taking no time or interest with their kids.

Therefore, it's no surprise that our kids are falling behind academically. Lack of parental involvement takes a huge toll. Kids who have help with homework, whose parents take a keen interest in what's going on at school, are the ones who do well, regardless of socioeconomic status. Study after study confirms it: if parents never appear at their kids' schools, if they are out of touch with their children's academic struggles, the kids simply don't do well academically.

The kids, unfortunately, follow their parents' cues. Many teens work long hours at jobs, even on school nights. It is common for kids to work solely to be able to buy the latest fashions, the best electronics, and a nice car. In the past, youngsters who worked did so to augment their parents' modest income, to save up for college, or to be able to go to the movies once a week with a date. Today, however, kids are so exhausted from working to have the "best" of everything that they often fall asleep in class.

But aren't after-school jobs a good idea? Is work one avenue for helping kids to learn? After all, working at an after-school job teaches valuable lessons about the "real" world. Why can't work be the answer for the struggling students of today?

Here's why. The work that young people can obtain nowadays is much less rewarding. The workplace is no longer filled with role models that will take the time to help youngsters learn a good work ethic and build good self-confidence. Today, the typical teen works at a fast-food restaurant, where virtually all their coworkers are other teens. They aren't learning from adults—they often don't even work with adults. Often, if they do work with adults, all they learn is more bad habits—how to cut corners, how to shortchange the company, how to value money above everything else.

Youngsters aren't being trained to stay with the company in the future; rather, they are viewed as expendable, a "necessary evil" to the employer. Parents may assume their teenagers are learning valuable skills at work, skills that will help them throughout their careers. But often the child is hired on the basis of skills he or she already has—such as good communication skills or punctuality—rather than being hired to learn new skills. Even the teens themselves do not see their jobs as being relevant to their future work. They aren't learning how to align their dreams with reality; they aren't getting guidance in making choices about careers or college, and they aren't being taken under the wing of a mentor. In short, kids just aren't getting it. And we will all pay for that in the future.

Often, too, teens are struggling with horrendous problems hidden painfully inside. The other students, the teachers, the coaches may never perceive the pressures, and the deep-seated issues a child may be struggling against. Many children are facing an uphill battle to survive—and this is true at every school in our country. No school is "typical" anymore—at least by the "old" definition of that word. What is typical is that kids are hurting. They need a better home life. They need understanding and guidance at school. They need help.

In the American classroom today, looks can be deceiving. The girl who refuses to participate in Spanish class may not be stubborn; she may be in despair because she's beaten regularly by her father. The boy laughing at the water fountain may be secretly struggling against the fear that his mother could lose her battle with cancer. The child from a financially strapped family may have to drop out of school and get a job to help his family survive. The jock who appears to have it all could be a drug addict. The kid with the wealthy parents might be getting lost in the shuffle as they move from state to state, from school to school, climbing the corporate ladder. This happens to poorer kids as well, as they are forced to move from place to place when evicted, or even to live on the streets or in homeless shelters. In either case, the result is a lack of stability and even identity—who am I going to be today and how will I relate to these strangers?

Without a strong internal compass, kids are losing their way. The rejection and taunting they may experience at school, the indifference or neglect they might find at home, the failure of all of us to see their needs and their pain are taking a tremendous toll on all of us.

What else is going on at our children's schools? Smoking. More kids are lighting up these days; in fact, smoking is at a 19-year high nationwide. In addition, over the past 10 years, the number of kids under 18 who became daily smokers each year has increased by over half a million—a greater than 70% increase. If these current trends continue, in Ohio (a typical state) alone, 285,000 kids now under 18 will eventually die from smoking. So blasé are schools about this that many have smoking rooms for the students.

Because of another insidious trend in which soft drink manufacturers provide schools that peddle their beverages with new scoreboards, scholarships, computer software and other "gifts," many kids will be swigging down that cola. What has happened to integrity? To putting kids first? Frankly, the schools can no longer afford to care about the student's receiving decent nutrition. They are so desperate for money that they have succumbed to the persuasion of these fat cat manufacturers.

## APATHY

Finally, these things all come together to produce a sense of futility in teachers. Don't try to teach, say seasoned educators. The support is gone!

One recent day I had a very interesting and shocking conversation with a current teacher. I asked this teacher if he felt that school systems were doing a good job of teaching our kids and if he felt the ability to teach was truly present.

His response was shocking. He said that when he first started teaching, he was excited to teach and engage the students as many other new teachers look forward to the same challenges and excitement. But, he said that as time progressed, he encountered many obstacles such as lack of support from administration, lack of involvement and support from parents, attitude of indifference, students' disrespect for authority, increase in violence, and his list went on and on. He said that when he was still in his early teaching years, he had a discussion with a veteran teacher about all his negative obstacles in teaching. The veteran teacher said to the younger teacher, "You won't believe what I am about to tell you, but in time you will agree and understand what I am saying."

Then the veteran teacher told the younger teacher, "If you want to survive in the teaching profession, then you have to give up doing one thing." The young teacher was on the edge of his seat and asked, "What is the one thing I need to stop doing?" The veteran teacher looked the younger teacher in his eyes and said, "You have to quit trying to teach." The younger teacher told me that he was shocked by this statement, but it was only a matter of time that he realized that, unfortunately, the veteran teacher was right.

The young teacher stated that the more he tried to do the job, the more resistance he encountered. This teacher said that many school administrators and teachers do care and want to do an effective job, but one by one they give up. He said that he got out of his teaching job and took an administrative job with the schools so that he didn't have to "teach" anymore.

We must all find ways to let our teachers teach and our students learn again.

**Chapter IV**

# School Rage: Saving Our Schools . . . and Our Kids

If we want kids to concentrate on their studies and if we want teachers to be able to focus on teaching, we've got to—once and for all—assure that schools are safe.

The good news is that a report prepared by the Department of Justice and the Department of Education did provide some hope. The report found that the overall crime rate in schools has dropped since 1993—good news, indeed. It also found that most schools are safer than the communities at large, despite the big-headline tragedies that fill our TV screens on a regular basis. Interestingly, the most violent crimes involving teenagers rarely occur in or near schools.

Not surprisingly, the report also found that violence is more likely in larger, urban schools. Hype aside, the most common school crimes are fist fights and theft, same as in the 1950s. But still there are the serious problems that lie behind situations such as those in Bethel, Alaska, and Joplin, Missouri, and these must be addressed.

Perhaps this decline in violence has been the result of initiatives that the schools and their communities have already begun. These fruitful ideas are ones that other school systems can put to use. One system, for instance, was having so many problems with violence that it instituted an entire series of remarkably effective solutions.

Clark County School District, responding to a gang shoot-out in a Las Vegas school, began a security program that has grown into a police organization that enforces the law as well as school rules, with a school police force aided by municipal police, business, and other school departments. The school police is a separate year-round department that fights crimes such as drugs and gang activity at sports events, and it tracks incidences and trends. It is trained in dealing with minors

The Clark County system includes several programs designed to reduce violence and intervene in crisis situations, and these, taken overall, represent many of the ways in which school districts are working to remedy the problem of school violence. Among these are:

- Operation Crime-Free School, which enlists students, community leaders, school and local police and federal enforcement agents to **cooperate**. It has produced several safety awareness guides for younger kids and a hotline for gathering information about crimes such as drugs, bomb threats, carrying weapons, vandalism and theft.
- Z-Squared, a zero weapons and **zero tolerance initiative** to teach offenders that offenses carry consequences and which publicizes both its rule and the need to do such things as keeping weapons secured away from kids. This program also helps secondary school teachers detect early warning signs of violence—lack of remorse, withdrawal, aggressive behavior, and difficulty controlling anger—and intervene in homicidal or suicidal

ideation. Teachers conduct class discussion and encourage contact with counselors and school police. It is hoped this information can be developed into a manual for the staff.

- **Peer mediation**, an increasingly popular idea, lets kids talk about disputes in private with a peer who has been trained to mediate solutions that are mutually determined and agreeable to both parties. This helps kids learn how to deal peacefully with differences of opinion and defuses hostility.

- Getting out, a program for teens, help them **to leave gangs** short of death or prison. Social services help gang members learn to live without gang support and there are even programs in which a local doctor helps them remove tattoos and other identifiers. To be in the program, youth must hold down a job, work with the police advisory unit and get counseling.

- An emergency crisis **management plan** outlines how all members of the school community, including students, should respond to violent situations such as a shooting, with emergency drills twice a year for staff.

These ideas are being used in part or full in many other areas of the country. Here is a general listing of some of the many ways schools are instituting measures to protect their young charges and teach them more acceptable ways to deal with problems:

## PHYSICAL SECURITY

A young father was proud of the school his little son attended, not because of its academic excellence, its beautiful grounds and play area, or even its championship baseball team. The measure of a good school, he implied, is found in its security measures. This seems to be a sign of the times.

Security measures are often seen as the primary way that

schools are dealing with school violence. Other schools use video cameras to monitor what's going on, and locked doors are legion. Communication is essential, as teachers and playground monitors have begun to carry walkie-talkies, and phones are installed in all classrooms. Some 53% of schools in 1999 said they maintain physical control of the entrances to their buildings, and some 4% said they use random metal detectors. Doorways and hallway guards, or at least a welcome desk at the door to monitor visitors, are one means of controlling access. These school guards can be school personnel, or, in 6% of cases, are actual full-time police officers.

Visitors in some schools, such as those in Hudson, Ohio, must wear their driver's license displayed on their bodies, while others have instituted the use of security badges for guests. Other schools—in the wake of school shootings— are moving polling places out of the school to keep visitors to a minimum, thereby depriving the students a sense that democracy is taking place under their noses and connecting them to society at large.

Some object that there are too many overt indications of security, saying they turn the school into an armed and uncomfortable camp. Others say that access control is key, arguing that it was a primary preventive of skyjackings. There must be some balance between creating a community friendly school and one that resembles a maximum-security lockup.

## SOCIETAL ISSUES

However, there are advocates who say that school safety must go far beyond metal detectors. They say that more resources must be targeted at children's needs, both educational and parental. Some want to expand what schools offer; others want to train parents better, and others want to assure that children are educated about more than the "three R's."

Colin Powell has said that there are five things we need to guarantee to make sure children are given the best start:

- An ongoing relationship with a caring adult: a mentor who says "I believe in you—and I demand you meet expectations for someone of your talents."
- A safe place with structured activities after school
- A healthy start physically
- A marketable skill through effective education and
- An opportunity to give back through community service.

Can we do all this, as a society? There is one organization called Fight Crime: Invest in Kids, a group of law enforcement officers and crime victims in Washington, D.C., that asks for solutions such as Head Start, parenting programs and other assistance to young parents with kids at high risk in inner city areas. In inner cities, they say, 98% of kids are killed outside schools, but after-school programs that offer recreation and education after 3 P.M., when kids are unsupervised and most at risk for trouble, could help. They want the restoration of educational "frills" such as music and art, sports and computer clubs for all kids—not just the good students—whom they believe need such services more.

There are also dozens of programs meant to help remedy today's problems and help parents learn and cope: early childhood education such as Parents as Teachers and First Step to Success that screen kids and help parents learn to deal with problem kids. There is also multi-systemic therapy, which offers parents an at-home program where therapists teach parents how to enforce rules, keep kids away from bad influences and help kids hook into support networks.

The American Medical Association Alliance fields a Stop America's Violence Everywhere program to work with communities to teach kids self-esteem and responsibility, as well as how to resolve anger constructively. The AMA asks parents to turn off violent TV, music and videogames, as well as to be good role models and to provide supervised after-school activities.

A healthy start is one method Colin Powell suggested as a

way to solve the problems of youth today. With this in mind, it is interesting to find out that one school eliminated fights, expulsions and suicides largely by offering students healthy foods in the cafeteria and not allowing them access to junk food. This was reported on by the World Future Society, which foresees better nutrition for students as one of the top 10 trends in its "Outlook 2002." For more on this, you can contact the society's Web site at www.wfs.org.

In addition to what the schools are doing, the kids themselves need to contribute to efforts to give them safe schools. At a White House Conference on School Safety, former President Clinton once said, "In too many schools, there is still too much disrespect for authority and still too much intolerance of other students from different backgrounds." These two factors speak volumes.

To remedy this, some are touting programs such as Character First to teach traditional values that kids are not learning in the home. They include lessons such as truthfulness, attentiveness, respect for authority, responsibility, orderliness and forgiveness. This clarifies a moral code for a generation whose parents were taught through values clarification to determine what constitutes righteous behavior and a good character by themselves. Good ideas, but some have said they are not being done in time to help this generation of kids today.

## ANTI-VIOLENCE PROGRAMS AT SCHOOL

At a higher level, many of today's high school students are being educated about violence prevention, as the Clark County kids are. In 1999, some 78% of schools had violence-prevention programs, either as one-day events or ongoing courses. Schools and parents are teaching kids on what to look for in their classmates—signs that have been demonstrated by the vast majority of perpetrators of school violence. These signs include interrupting others, flaunting one's authority or status in a condescending manner, belittling someone's opinion, giving others the "silent treatment," verbal sexual harassment, staring or dirty looks, intentionally putting down someone's work, and insulting, yelling and shouting at others. The schools and parents work with the kids on what to do when confronted by this kind of behavior.

Some schools also find an answer in behavioral reforms, such as requiring uniforms, which 3% of schools had done in 1999; others are banning backpacks that can be used to carry contraband or stolen items. Others, 80% of schools, now require students to stay in the school and not leave at lunchtime as a security measure.

In one violence-prevention program, kids learn a variety of lessons. There is self-control time that helps them guard against rage, a pledge to create a positive classroom climate, games and discussions that help them internalize confidence, and a chance to work together to learn to resolve conflicts. Students also learn to take responsibility for their actions and to understand their consequences. The lessons are part of the Skills for Life program developed by the Lesson One Foundation, based in Boston, which has taken them into elementary schools for the last two decades.

The idea behind it, according to founder Jon Oliver, is that kids need to learn very early in life to respect themselves and others, to control their impulses, and to know that anger need not always be acted upon. High school, he notes, is far too late to begin developing these skills and attitudes.

Other schools are insisting that students must also learn to be accountable and responsible for their actions. One preventive measure includes an educational effort that teaches students that bullying is wrong. Students must learn to accept and respect students of all races, religions, genders, national origins, sexual orientations and even degrees of "coolness." While there will always be some name calling and cliquishness in schools, it should not be so pervasive as to target specific individuals in an unremitting display.

## ANTI-BULLYING EFFORTS

Perhaps the biggest behavioral change for students has been in efforts to teach kids not to bully. Some say that bullying has always been a problem in school, and that is true. It seems to have escalated and gotten more serious, becoming a normal part of the day and so inherent that it is not even fought against or discouraged. But, in the wake of reports from schools with names like Santana and Columbine, that is rapidly changing.

Rich Harvell, president of the North American School Safety and Law Enforcement Officers group, said educators have to institute no tolerance for bullying strategies at the various schools. In addition, schools must create a means by which students can report bullying and a way to follow up. It is important that schools create a means to explore every report of trouble.

Government is also working on solutions to bullying. Lawmakers in states including Texas, New York and Massachusetts, are working on anti-bullying legislation that would include early intervention and counseling to automatic expulsion of offenders. And, in the aftermath of a death caused by a bully in Georgia, Gov. Roy Barnes signed an anti-bullying law in 1999 calling for expulsion for three-time offenders. Gov. Gary Locke of Washington State asked for mandatory anti-bullying training in schools.

While legislators and executives act, law is also at work in another way to stop bullying. Two parents, Karrie and Ken Laugstad, sued the bully who harassed and tormented their wheelchair-using daughter, along with the school district that they felt was negligent in its supervision.

Parents are working in other ways to stop bullies. One mother of a victim, Jenny Wieland, of Seattle, Washington, in 1994 started Mothers Against Violence in America, a group patterned after Mothers Against Drunk Drivers. She has since become the first director of Students Against Violence Everywhere, an organization with 126 student-led chapters that offer anti-harassment and conflict-resolution programs.

This is all to the good for society, but what can you do to protect your own child? First, look for signs that your child is being bullied or is a bully, say the experts. According to clinical psychologist Dr. William Porter, a co-author of a book published by Cherry Creek School District in Colorado called *Bully-Proofing Your School*, victims may be unwilling to go to school, have damage to self or possessions that they do not want to explain, and are silent and depressed.

Dr. Porter suggests that parents respond by drawing the child out, listening to their fears, expressing confidence that the problem is resolvable, while all the time trying to find someone at the school to help. Parent and child can practice protective skills such as using humor to deflect tension or avoiding confrontation. Parents of bullies, he says, should set clear and consistent expectations of behavior, work with the school to follow up, find positive ways to give the child the attention he or she is seeking, and not let the child wangle his way out of responsibility for the behavior, which is a common practice with bullies.

## SCHOOL AND CLASS SIZE

Teachers often cite larger class sizes as a major factor in disrespect and intolerance. They feel that having smaller classes will enable them to become aware of troubled children sooner and to find help for them before they become violent. To do this, we need many more teachers, along with the money to pay them, and the money to provide modernized and enlarged schools, as well as better teacher training, especially training to find and stop bullies.

It is said that high schools work best when there are only 600 to 900 students enrolled. Fewer students mean few are marginalized and more kids get to indulge in after-school programs with an adult role model. One promising idea is to restructure schools into smaller elements, where kids have a better sense of identification with and pride in their schools.

They get to know the other students better as people. And teachers get to know them. Teachers stay with pupils longer, so they can identify the potential troublemakers.

Small, more intimate school settings are important because the Secret Service has just released a study which shows that school shooters always planned the attacks ahead of time—and discussed them with others in a majority of instances. Eric Harris had planned for a year to bomb Columbine High and kill 500 classmates, it was found.

With smaller schools, it is argued, teachers are more likely to know what is going on and to hear reports of trouble, as well as to elicit more trust from students. The Secret Service study looked at 37 school shootings since 1974 that involved 41 shooters, of which 25 were interviewed. It was found that "there was no instance where the attack in a school was impulsive, said agent Bryan Vossefull, who is the co-director of the agency's Safe School Initiative. In addition, the attacks all had targeted specific students.

## Early Warnings

The Secret Service study suggests that school shootings can be prevented, as the attackers had, by a large majority, done something before the shooting to attract the attention of a teacher, schoolmate or police officer. There was no profile of the typical shooter, as perpetrators ranged from 11 to 21, and they were of all races and economic backgrounds. But most of the shooters, two-thirds, had been bullied before the incident.

It is sometimes hard to say just what can be done when presented with the facts about a possible shooting. Littleton's Harris had boasted on his Web site about the bombs and threatened to kill one classmate, Brooks Brown, by name, along with many others, indicating also how little he cared about his own life. The Browns took the threat to the attention of the authorities, but the information was not taken to a judge so that direct action could be taken. The local sheriff said that because the Browns would not swear out a complaint, the elements of a crime could not be established. When his parents were informed of his postings, Harris was able to convince his father that the words were just idle threats. The boys were put into a special program to divert them from violence.

Indeed, many lawsuits have been threatened by the families of school shooting victims because the schools and enforcement authorities have known about the danger posed by the shooter and they did nothing. Even the Klebolds, the family of Harris' partner in the Littleton shooting, are suing because they feel that someone, anyone, should have put a rein on Harris.

Kip Kinkel's parents tried desperately to help him, with medications, teacher conferences and juvenile detention, until he murdered them and shot 24 others. Sometimes, no matter how hard you try, there is no way to address certain mental illnesses with education.

## Gun Manufacture and Availability

Guns are a problem, when they are found in schools. How can we make them safer? First, we can manufacture guns with an emphasis on safety innovations instead of making them more deadly. Many needed safety features are readily available and inexpensive, such as a load indicator that indicates whether the firearm is loaded and a magazine disconnect safety to keep the gun from firing if the magazine is removed. Childproofing and personalizing guns is relatively simple, requiring only a locking mechanism to prevent unauthorized users from firing it.

Guns also need to be designed for civilian use rather than criminal use, such as assault weapons and low-quality Saturday Night Specials. There is no need for cop-killer bullets and mail-order parts so guns can be assembled without serial numbers. Advertising should be realistic about gun fatalities and focus on features other than the fingerprint-resistant finish. Finally, guns should be more safely distributed and sold only to those of age and not through gun shows or other unregulated venues.

All of the Littleton weapons came from a gun show, and three of the four were purchased by an 18-year-old legally able to buy there for the perpetrators.

There is no need for guns to be unsafe. Cars, swimming pools and poorly made or designed toys also kills kids, but we at least try to keep this from happening through the vigilance of agencies such as the Consumer Product Safety Commission. Only firearms are completely exempt from efforts to create safer weapons. Yet, guns create far more havoc and horror than do lawn darts, peanuts in the lunchroom, toxic playgrounds and other things that have society writhing in horror.

Only 11 kids died in 1999 in car trunks, yet car makers were respondent to concerns about this and installed inside-trunk latches to alleviate the problem, even going so far as to research what kinds of latches would be most easy to operate by children. Guns continue to be made more lethal, even to those who use them.

Gun control laws do work. Child access prevention laws passed in 17 states hold gun owners criminally liable if kids use the guns to hurt themselves or others, and accidental death of children in the states where this law was in effect decreased by 23% in the two years after.

## Guns in Schools

In schools, we can "sniff out" guns . . . and bombs and drugs . . . before they harm anyone. In Orleans Parish, Louisiana, a team of gun-sniffing dogs goes to 37 secondary schools on a daily basis. Although they do find guns in schools, the dogs are even more valuable in deterring kids from bringing guns to school. Area school districts reported that gun incidents in schools dropped by nearly 50% during a recent school year. Other schools insist that metal detectors are keeping the guns out, though many parents and students object to the devices being used in schools because of the atmosphere they create.

There is a major link that has been found between drug use

and violence in schools, and the risk and protective factors for teen drug use and violence are largely the same. In other words, preventing drug use goes a long way toward preventing other violent behavior. Dr. J. David Hawkins, Ph.D., has found that communities that had assessed their risk factors for drugs and adopted programs proven to work against them have not only reduced teen drug use, but other delinquent behaviors, such as violence, as well. The two go hand in hand.

Therefore, schools are also instituting zero tolerance programs for weapons, along with zero tolerance programs for drugs, as another way to fight guns and violence in schools. Zero tolerance programs are also useful in dealing with bullying, keeping victims from becoming killers.

Although some say that these have been carried to extremes when they start targeting kindergarteners drawing pictures of soldiers, a good zero tolerance program, such as the one in Clark County, Nevada, tells students that there are predetermined consequences for specific offenses such as possession of firearms and then enforces them. These consequences can include expulsion and placement in special schools for problem students. There were more than 5,000 student expulsions due to possession of firearms in schools in 1996-97. And 3,300 schools moved problem students to special programs that year.

## HOT-LINES

Are there ways to enlist the aid of teenagers in putting a stop to the proliferation of firearms—or of other anti-social behaviors? Many grass roots programs are showing promise, including one that has proven successful in Boston, MA, Akron, OH, and Charleston, SC. Youngsters can anonymously phone the Gun Tip Hotline to report other children who have possession of firearms. After a gun is confiscated, the reporting youngster is rewarded with $100, usually bestowed at the caller's home or another designated place. Funding for the programs come from donations, particularly from churches. The hotline program is saving children's lives, including the lives of the youngsters carrying the guns. Tragedy can be averted . . . with a concerted effort on everyone's part.

This kind of call-in line is known as "crime stoppers'" line as it rewards callers. Most states have them to receive tips on all kinds of violence. However, some activists, such as the ACLU, worry that this kind of anonymous tip can be used vindictively and without accountability.

Another kind of hotline that is seen as an answer to getting more information about what is going on in schools at the student level is a "safe school" line. One company that operates such lines for school districts is the Columbus, Ohio-based Security Voice, Inc. It contracts with schools to let callers leave tips or rumors on an 800 number about violent activity that is being planned. The company then relays the message to schools to see if action is warranted. Callers receive a code number so they can call back and find out what action has been taken. Such "safe schools" hotlines, which can operate by voice or fax, have been a success, with 20% of calls dealing with drug activity, followed by general safety issues or weapons. They do not offer rewards but do allow a means for feedback, and they would be a good way for students being bullied to report problems.

## LEGAL REMEDIES

Everywhere, legislators are stepping in to make schools safer from violence. Schools in some states are mandated to have a clear crisis management plan for each building in the district that can be followed in any kind of emergency, natural or social. These are being developed by coalitions including administrators, teachers, parents, cops, firefighters, administrators, the FBI and hazardous materials professionals, much as the people in Clark Country have done.

Laws have also called for areas around schools to be called safety zones or drug free zones, where penalties are heavier for criminal behavior. School districts in some areas can punish students for carrying guns or knives at school functions off the school grounds and keep students who were expelled from enrolling elsewhere.

In at least 11 states, as well as in the Supreme Court and in Congress, government entities have bought a computer-assisted threat assessment system to rank the potential for violence of any threatening person, such as a stalker or terrorist. Some companies worried about workplace violence are also using such devices to diagnose problems so they can intervene after a suspicious person has shown early signs of trouble. Some states, such as Ohio, are considering using such a system in schools, and the manufacturers have included information from 18 school fatalities to help determine risk factors in educational settings.

There are some other promising new initiatives being discussed in Washington, and at grass roots levels throughout the U.S, including: a School Emergency Response to Violence project to help schools respond to school-related violent deaths; a program for training and hiring up to 2,000 community police and school resource officers to work in high-crime schools; programs to help develop better school safety programs; and a joint effort between MTV and the federal government to launch a campaign to encourage young people to become mentors, helping younger children to learn conflict resolution skills.

## THE MOUTHS OF BABES

Can the kids themselves offer solutions to school rage? You bet. In summits on youth violence, in cafeteria discussions, in churches, and on the streets, teenagers get to the heart of the matter . . . and their message can be summed up in simple terms: Parents should spend more time with their children and do a better job of instilling values.

At a conference in Colorado, following the tragic Columbine High School shootings, young people met with clergy, youth workers, and an array of experts—and spoke from the heart. One teen, Julian Gilbert, said: "The reason I turned out good is I was blessed with a mother who still built me up, regardless of what other people thought of me. That's what a lot of parents need to do."

Other teens attending the meeting ignored the raging national debate over cultural decline, the impact of violent movies, and the easy access to guns and returned repeatedly to a simple message: Parents need to be more supportive, more caring, and more nurturing. Is anyone listening?

For more on the topic of talking to, and listening to, kids, go to *www.talkinghwithkids.org.*

**Chapter V**

# WORK RAGE: WHEN CO-WORKERS "GO POSTAL"

All your life, you planned to work for a good company. You went to school, learned a trade, pounded the pavement and finally worked your way into a decent job. And when you got there, what did you see?

Perhaps you saw a company with workers and managers who care—a productive and committed team. But, even if your work environment appears okay on the surface, it is becoming increasingly likely that there is still an unseen and unknown hostility which may be brewing: seemingly normal coworkers, who, at any moment, may snap, and "go postal." They might threaten, abuse, intimidate, harass, bully, or even murder those around them.

Workplace violence in all of its forms is now rated the number one security threat to America's workers, according to Pinkerton's Sixth Annual "Top Security Threats Facing Corporate America." It is estimated that approximately 30% of violent incidents involve current or former employees. We simply cannot afford to ignore workplace anger . . . it will and has come back to haunt us.

Every day, there are new examples of workplace violence. According to Justice Department statistics, more than one million U.S. workers become victims of workplace assaults each year. Most frightening is that the FBI says cases of employees physically attacking or killing their co-workers have doubled in the last decade.

Some of the more infamous U.S. workplace killings in the 1990s include:

- November 3, 1999: a yet to be identified gunman kills two and wounds two others at a repair shop in Seattle.
- November 2, 1999: XEROX copy repairman Brian Uyesugi, 40, allegedly kills seven co-workers in Honolulu. He surrenders after a five-hour standoff.
- August 5, 1999: Truck driver Allan Miller, 34, allegedly kills three current and former co-workers. He is awaiting trial.
- July 29, 1999: Investor Mark O. Barton, 44, kills nine people and wounds 13 others at two brokerage firms in Atlanta, then kills himself.
- March 6, 1998: Matthew Beck, 35, a Connecticut Lottery accountant involved in a pay dispute, kills the lottery president and three others before killing himself.
- December 18, 1997: Arturo Reyes Torres, 43, kills his former boss and three other people at a maintenance yard in Orange, California. Torres, who blamed the supervisor for getting him fired, is killed by police.
- September 15, 1997: Fired assembly line worker Arthur H. Wise allegedly opens fire at a Aiken, South Carolina parts plant, killing four and wounding four others and wounding three others. He is awaiting trial.
- June 5, 1997: Daniel S. Mardsen, 38, a plastics factory employee in Santa Fe Springs, California, kills two co-

workers and wounds four others in an argument. He kills himself less than two hours later.

- April 3, 1995: James Simpson, 28, a former employee at a refinery inspection in Corpus Christi, Texas, kills the owner of the company, his wife, and three workers before shooting himself to death.
- March 14, 1994: Tuan Nguyen, 29, recently fired from a Santa Fe Springs, California electronics factory, shoots three people to death before killing himself.
- December 2, 1993: Alan Winterbourne, 33, an unemployed computer engineer, opens fire in an unemployment office in Oxnard, California, killing three state workers and injuring four others. He later kills a police officer. The police then kill him.
- July 1, 1993: Gian Luigi Ferri, a mentally disturbed man with a grudge against lawyers, opens fire in a San Francisco law office, killing eight people and then himself.
- June 18, 1990: James E. Pough goes on a shooting spree in General Motors Acceptance Corp. office in Florida, killing 10 people and wounding four others before killing himself. GMAC had just repossessed his car.

In a November 1999 survey, more than half of U.S. companies have experienced at least one incident of workplace violence in the past three years, according to the Society for Human Resource Management in Arlington, Virginia. The survey found that shootings and stabbings accounted for 2% of incidents. The most common violent acts were verbal acts (41%) and "pushing and shoving" (29%).

The study, compiled from surveys filled out by human resource managers at 681 companies, found that 55% of the incidents involved "personality conflicts" between employees. Only 8% were directed by an employee against his or her supervisor.

In 76% of the cases, the aggressors were men, and in 45%,

the victims were women. Firings were the catalyst for only 18% of the violent incidents, while work-related stress accounted for 24%.

One of the most horrifying incidences was the Atlanta shooting rampage of Mark Barton, a seemingly normal securities day trader who opened fire on the employees of two brokerage firms, killing nine and wounding 13 before committing suicide. As authorities struggle to establish a motive for the tragedy, people throughout the country began to wonder, "Could that happen here?"

The answer, unfortunately, is "yes." It could happen in any community, at any time. Random acts of violence in the workplace are happening with alarming regularity. The phrase, "Counselors will be available at XYZ Company today to help employees process their reactions to the killings that recently took place at the firm ..." is becoming chillingly too familiar to working Americans.

The carnage is widespread ... and getting worse. Meanwhile, the growing incidence of workplace murders is just part of the story. Christine McGovern, a workplace violence expert, estimates that one million workers—18,000 a week!—become victims of nonfatal workplace assaults each year. Her "Ten Most Peculiar Reasons Employees Assault Coworkers" catalogs the range of workplace violence incidents occurring today:

- A supervisor who didn't like an employee placed cockroaches inside the lid of the woman's hairspray bottle. When the employee opened the bottle, she was so startled by the cockroaches that she suffered a heart attack.
- A janitor, enraged that his paycheck was late, poured gasoline on the company's bookkeeper and set her on fire.
- A terminated employee karate-chopped the woman who hired him, breaking every bone in her jaw and leaving her with only four teeth.

- A dishwasher threw an empty beer keg at his co-worker whom he believed was talking about him behind his back.
- An office supervisor was choked and his glasses knocked off for denying a woman her unemployment claim.

Beyond murder and physical assault, "bullying" is becoming an escalating workplace issue. We all remember the schoolyard bullies who made our life miserable in grade school. Fortunately, most of these aggressive troublemakers later grew up to be solid citizens. But today, experts are concerned about a new brand of bullying which is becoming an alarming trend in America's workplace. Just as the Columbine High School tragedy had some of its roots in "cliquishness" and bullying—both endured and committed by the perpetrators of the crimes—so, too, is the workplace becoming the site of frequent psychological and physical intimidation.

About 22% of all U.S. workers have been bullied at work, says a Wayne State University study, and a Columbia University study found nine of 10 workers have had a bullying bosses. Some 70% of bullies are men, and in 89% of cases, they outrank the victim—in only 4.5% of cases was the bully of lower rank. They bully about half the time in public. Some 31% of bullies do it because the victims refuse to be subservient, 21% because they are jealous of the victim's skills, 14% because it is the workplace culture, 18% for unprovoked reasons and 16% of the time for other reasons. Victims respond by worrying, missing work, reducing time at work or even changing jobs.

British author Tim Field discovered firsthand how devastating the effects of workplace bullying can be. After a successful 15-year career in computer systems and support, Field got a new boss who criticized, threatened and intimidated him. He overruled Field's decisions and undermined his confidence to the point that Field ultimately suffered a stress breakdown. He states that bullying is far more serious and widespread than previously documented. Field believes employers should increase their awareness of the types of bullying that take place at work and help their employees develop strategies for coping and reducing its incidence.

A distinction can be drawn between "harassment," which can be an isolated incident, and "bullying," which, by definition involves repeated incidents and often a pattern of behavior. Bullying often occurs when a clique forms and begins to pick on others. The Littleton tragedy was strongly linked to bullying, taunting, and harassment. One dilemma in resolving such problems, in both schools and the workplace, is that those in charge often don't realize the seriousness of the problem until it is too late.

Employers, in particular, tend to dismiss inappropriate behavior unless it involves a contract dispute or legal action. However, the bottom line is that bullying is very much a part of the workplace landscape, even though we would like to think it happens only in schools.

In addition to intimidation and psychological aggression, bullying includes vandalism, gestures, withholding of important work-related information. In short, bullying can be very subtle. "Serial" bullies—those who engage in aggression regardless of circumstances, rather than simply in response to a specific situation—are becoming increasingly prevalent. They are quite dangerous individuals because they are usually introverted, intelligent, and hard to detect.

"Bullying" is loosely defined, then, as repeated aggressive behavior that deliberately causes physical or psychological torment. It's now seen as a "silent epidemic" affecting our offices and factories.

Loraleigh Keashly, an associate professor of urban and labor studies at Wayne State University in Detroit, calls bullying "very much a part of the workplace experience," which explodes the popular American misperception that bullying is just a schoolyard problem. Keashly notes that psychological aggression in the workplace is misread. The media, for instance, "gives the impression that physical violence is the norm in the workplace, when, in reality, the more subtle bullying behaviors occur with greater frequency.

Another ugly form of workplace warfare—employee sabotage—is occurring with greater and greater frequency in America. *Webster's Dictionary* defines "sabotage" as "deliberate destruction of machines, etc., by employees," but that's just the tip of the iceberg in today's work world. Employee sabotage is nothing short of a nightmare.

We may think of sabotage as internal theft of an employee stealing products from the company (example: a stereo system), but it's more complicated than that. Even if we consider theft alone, the numbers are staggering. A 1993 survey that compared the theft losses in retail stores examined how much money and product was stolen by employees, as compared to thefts by shoplifters. The results were staggering. Amazingly, employee theft accounted for up to 94% of the total amount of loss.

I am convinced many employees firmly believe in what I call the pocket theory. If the item belonging to the company they work for fits in their pocket, then it is acceptable to steal (or should we say borrow forever) the item because the company can "darn well afford it" and "I work hard and don't get all that I am worth from this company." This attitude continues to spread and grow today in more and more businesses than ever in the history of corporate America. My company investigated and solved a $600,000.00 embezzlement for a Fortune 100 company and it was from a key salaried employee who was paid well. Evidently, the employee felt that he deserved more money.

This destructive tendency, seen in resentful, angry, bitter employees, is costing corporate America a bundle. Disgruntled workers erase databases, tamper with products, steal money—and the list goes on. Employee sabotage is exacting a huge toll in time and money from employers of all sizes. More important, beyond the economic cost, is the fact that sabotage can also be very dangerous and can endanger the lives of coworkers.

Many small business owners believe that embezzlements

and major thefts only happen to the bigger businesses. This is far from the truth. I have had a six-person dentist's office administrator embezzle $35,000 in only 3 months. I have had a family-run lumber-supply company foreman steal company supplies and gas. I have had employees from manufacturing companies steal valuable scrap metal, tools, food, engine parts, products, etc. The greatest indication of how sad the situation is is that almost all companies with power tools that are used inside their businesses, warehouses and manufacturing areas will have this "fenced and locked cage of security" sitting right in the middle of their working area where employees have to sign power tools and replacement parts in and out. This is supposed to be a place where employees are friends and "trust" each other? When I review company policy with business executives who believe that they have no problems inside their businesses, I find out that all the lockers have locks, file drawers are locked up, offices are locked and the list goes on. I often wonder, what really is our definition of a "great place to work?"

There are some places that give signs of hope. I was called one day to discuss with one company's employees options for increasing personal security. I was shocked to hear what had taken place there. This manufacturing company never had a theft, but recently, they had a car broken into, a radio stolen and some money taken from a desk. All the employees got together and took up a collection to pay for the stolen radio and stolen money. Now, they wanted to know how to improve and prevent theft from happening again. This was a very refreshing day for me and my line of business.

## BLASTING BAD BACKGROUNDS

Employers lose thousands of dollars per year hiring employees with bad backgrounds. With 5,000 Americans trying cocaine for the first time every day in the U.S., what is the worst mistake an employer can make? Is it drug testing and background checks and invasions of privacy?

I don't think so, and here's an example taken from my own files to explain why.

A disability-retired police officer from Akron, Ohio started his own auto parts business. It was his longtime dream, but after only five years in business, he was going bankrupt because his key employee, disabled in a motorcycle accident, repaid his kindness by stealing him blind.

In another case, a company executive couldn't figure out why the work wasn't done on the night shift . . . until a private investigator revealed drugs smuggled in with the cleaning people at night. Employees use a variety of shocking methods to sneak drugs and alcohol, and employers have several options in dealing with that problem.

Here's one way: When Branch Roofing, Inc., located in Akron, Ohio, decided to put money second to ethical and moral concerns by beginning drug testing, they lost two-thirds of their workforce. But by offering rehabilitation instead of prosecution, they gained a reputation for being a good employer, as well as a 100% drug-free workplace in the end. It nearly cost them their entire company's existence while they worked it all out.

Unfortunately, no company is immune to threat of theft, drugs and sabotage. Acts of workplace sabotage can range from deliberate nonperformance to financial fraud. Angry employees have set buildings on fire, put rodents into food products, and concealed needles in baby food. We can all recall the drug tampering incidents of a few years ago that ultimately cost manufacturers a bundle in lost consumer confidence and redesigned, tamper-proof packaging.

Sabotage in the workplace usually doesn't only involve physical violence, however. Instead, in many cases, it tends to be misconduct triggered by a need for revenge. This type of activity can hurt companies, far more than broken windows or stolen pens, because it damages the company's reputation and image.

Sabotage in the workplace usually takes two forms. The first kind is done politically to damage careers, a company's professional image or credibility. The second type of sabotage is done physically, to hurt the company or co-workers.

What's the motive? Advancing one's own career by making others look bad, or trying to hurt an individual to get even for real or perceived mistreatment.

The American workplace today is a perfect incubator for employee sabotage. Employees are full of rage and frustration. They are disheartened and angered by knowing that the company feels no loyalty to them, that they can be downsized or laid off at any time. They are often managed by individuals who lack the skills for the job. They feel disenfranchised, unheard of and unimportant by their co-workers. All of this contributes to a dangerous environment at work.

Some forms of employee misconduct also work against the corporation's success. Employees may sabotage the company by purposely refusing to work up to expectations. Lost productivity is tremendously costly to employers, and these angry employees know it. Also, managers may agree to carry out the boss' wishes, while privately having no intention of doing so.

Some experts believe that sabotage is a symptom of boredom, overwork, or unresolved grievances. People with big beefs against the boss, the company, or their co-workers may see sabotage as a way by which they can gain leverage on their employers.

Downsizing—and how it is done—fuels some of the rage that leads to employee sabotage. If companies deliver the bad news in an uncaring, brusque way, the employee may look for revenge. On the other hand, companies that deal with this issue in more humane, caring ways are less likely to experience retribution.

Just how bad is this entire issue of downsizing? Every day, from 2000 to 3000 people lose their job; three-quarters of households have been affected with layoff since 1980, while 19 million people found joblessness had caused a major life crisis, according to Department of Labor statistics. We have created many names—downsizing, rightsizing, restructuring, reengineering, redirectment, degrowing, dehiring, redundancy elimination, workforce imbalance, redeployment, decruitment, personnel reduction, and so on—to cushion this negative impact of being laid off in hopes that we could take the bite out of this situation. To our dismay, it has hardly helped. In reality, the situation has only gotten worse.

My company has seen a significant increase in requests for us to provide assistance in terminating employees. These requests are not regular requests, but rather requests that we be "armed" during layoffs just in case there is a problem. If the risk is viewed as potentially harmful, then we are assigned to remain armed on company premises for several months. Think about this new trend that requires outside professionals to be present and be armed to terminate a current employee. The former employee is now the current potential enemy.

We know that employee sabotage is on the rise. Computer-related crime, for example, is increasingly done by the company's own staff (or former employees). In its recent "Intellectual Property Loss Special Report," the American Society for Industrial Security reported that 89% of respondents said that their biggest concern about system security was retaliation by disgruntled employees. Security experts warn that the greatest threat to databases in the future will come from within, rather than from outside hackers.

Here are some other scary statistics:

- Employee turnover is at an all-time high, and about 60% of workers want to change jobs in the next year. Turnover causes many problems, from a lack of continuity and psychological investment in the workplace to work inefficiencies and resulting frustration on the part of experienced workers who cannot count on new hires.
- Some 75% of workers are not happy with work. About 29% of workers have yelled at colleagues and 23% have

cried at work due to stress. Gallup says that in a global survey, 80% of employees say they do not get the chance to do what they do best every day.

- Employers have seen a 36% increase in the number of job applicants who are not eligible for rehire due to personality conflicts, disciplinary issues, theft and embezzlement. Many also lack basic reading and writing skills. The American Management Association says that over 38% of 1999 job applicants lacked the skills needed to do the job, up from 35.5% in 1998 and 22.8% in 1997.

## REASONS BEHIND THE RISE OF VIOLENCE IN THE WORKPLACE

The nature of the workplace today is one of the greatest sources for the problems that eventually lead to violence against co-workers. Here's a look at just some of the realities facing today's worker: harassment, demoralization, the changing composition of the workforce, overwhelming technology, lack of privacy, and always-worried upper-management.

Incidents of harassment, now being tracked more effectively, have been increasing at a rate of 300% per year. Sexual harassment cases have been widely publicized, but the more insidious verbal harassment and aggressive behavior are more often the more prevalent form. Caught in a quandary, companies often choose to make a settlement and seldom fire the alleged harasser, for fear of risking a wrongful termination suit or even violent retaliation.

Many workers are demoralized by news about high CEO salaries, and by managers who seem more concerned about their "golden parachutes" than about building a productive team. The ratio for CEO to common worker pay in 2000 was 531:1, an unbelievable amount. The Japanese ratio was 11:1.

Also, these same workers experience an ever-worsening time crunch between their work and home lives. This problem is so prevalent that President Clinton, during his presidency, recently proposed federal programs to help working parents take more time for their children. Citing a study conducted by key economic advisors, the president said American workers are suffering because they have far less time to spend with their families than the previous generation's workers. He warned that "unless we act now, that problem will get worse." Parents should not have to fear losing their job because they left work to take a sick child to the doctor. They should not have to call in sick in order to be able to attend a parent-teacher conference at their child's school.

Today's workplace is as diverse a "melting pot" as the country as a whole. There are more women, disabled persons, immigrants, and aging workers employed than ever before. Building tolerance, understanding and sensitivity between these workers must be a key concern among the upper management of any corporation—and yet, to date, few companies are addressing these issues sufficiently.

The world doesn't sleep anymore. The dramatically increasing use of the Internet and the need for companies to compete globally creates around-the-clock work environments. Overwhelming technology makes this possible. The number of workers with home computers has increased significantly, and this often translates into workers taking more work home and having even less time for themselves and with their families, adding to the pressure of the employee. Multimedia interconnectivity has made it easier to communicate, but also harder for employees to distinguish who is really accountable.

According to the Society for Human Resource Management, the workplace is emerging as a critical battleground in the fight for privacy rights. Technology has allowed employers (and potential employers) access to intimate details of their employees' and candidates' lives. A Harris poll showed 89% of Americans are concerned about invasions of their privacy in this manner.

The tight squeeze between keeping employees happy and motivated and implementing cost-cutting procedures makes for some extremely worried managers. On the one hand, they are expected to meet or exceed company goals, which usually relate to finding ways to do more with fewer employees. On the other hand, they are expected to carry responsibility for molding employees into happy, productive workers. There's little room for balance. This creates a pressure cooker for the manager who recognizes that you cannot force the fit. Many fine managers, feeling that their hands are tied, often quit rather than try to meet impossible demands. This creates a "brain drain," more frustration in the remaining employees, and a lack of continuity for the corporation.

One of the seeds of countless workplace problems that come from outside of the workplace environment is depression. We are only now beginning to understand and acknowledge for the first time the major impact of depression on the workplace environment. Depression afflicts some 19 million Americans each year. This is an expensive problem in the workplace, costing businesses up to $44 billion annually in absenteeism, treatment costs, mortality and productivity loss, according to mental health experts.

A survey sponsored by the Society for Human Resource Management and the National Foundation for Brain Research, found that 8 out of 10 human resource professionals report identifying depression in one or more of their employees over the past three years. Notes Paul Greenberg, director of the Analysis Group's Health Care Economics Practice in Cambridge, Massachusetts, "The effect [of depression] on a person's career path and their lifetime earnings is enormous."

In the workplace, most employers don't seem to understand that it benefits the company to treat depressed employees. The cost to the company of untreated illness is far higher than the cost of treatment. Today, the treatment of depression is still too often viewed as a cost to be managed, rather than as an investment.

Today, companies are just beginning to realize the scope of workplace violence mitigated by depression. The horrific cases of depressed workers running amok and beating or killing customers or co-workers are becoming more and more common. Beyond the more sensationally reported cases, incidents occur every day and hardly anybody even pays attention:

- A violence-prone tool distribution worker in North Carolina who had failed to take his medication kills two.
- At a trucking terminal in Arkansas, a worker who was scheduled for his first therapy session the next day kills his boss and then himself.
- In Ohio, an estranged husband guns down his wife in the parking lot of her company, in front of her stunned co-workers.
- In Pelham, Alabama, a man goes to work and shoots two of his co-workers to death. Then he goes to another company, where he had previously been employed, and kills a third person. The man is found not guilty by reason of insanity and sentenced to undergo "extensive treatment for manic depression at the Alabama State Hospital."

Another seed for rage in the workplace is our ever-more desensitized society. We're all too familiar with the profile of a guy who shuts out others who seem to be on friendly terms with "the enemy." He then begins having fantasies of "putting them in their place." Finally, he appears at work one day with a loaded shotgun and begins emptying rounds at everyone. Is he responsible, or is he a symptom?

We've become desensitized as a society by violence, and we see aggression erupting everywhere. We have words for it, too, like "Going postal." Violence is so prevalent, now it's in the workplace and just another part of our culture of rage. There are nearly two million workplace violence incidents each year in this country—and we're not alone—many other countries are experiencing the same dangerously explosive situations in factories, shops and office buildings. There's more bad news. The U.S. has the most potentially lethal outbursts of any country in the world. And, we have placed ourselves, unknowingly, at the top of the list when it comes to violence against our fellow workers.

To put a finger on the pulse of what is happening in today's workplace, just look closely at the newspaper. Each and every week, an average of 20 people is murdered at work. Another 18,000 are assaulted. It doesn't even make the headlines anymore. It rates just a column or a paragraph on the second or third page. Managers tell pollsters that dealing with employee conflict and dealing with personnel problems are their biggest time wasters. Should assaults be acceptable as the cost of doing business?

Every day there is another news item telling the same story. We search for answers. We want to know why and how anything like this could happen. Workplaces are supposed to be about business. They are presumed to be safe places, but as we've seen in our schools, churches, hospitals and office buildings across the country, Life Rage has infiltrated and spread its venom everywhere. No place is truly safe in America today.

## WHAT TO DO ABOUT WORK RAGE

Even though extremely violent crimes in the workplace seem to be decreasing, they are still very serious matters that must be avoided whenever possible. In addition, there are a number of less serious events, everyday kinds of things that can hamper workplace performance, breed lawsuits, and make life at work an outrage for many workers. These are things such as verbal abuse, threats, harassment, and stalking.

As things stand now, we can expect to see rage in the workplace continue, unless we can address some of these problems in society as a whole, However, there are some things that offices and workers can do in the short-term to create a more positive and supportive situation.

The first, perhaps, is to put an end to office bullying. Here are some basic tips about what companies can do:

1. Take verbal and written stances on all forms of workplace altercations, whether minor verbal abuse up to major incidences such as violence.
2. Create a process for reporting bullying, including who to direct the complaints to, allowing the company to conduct an objective and thorough investigation. An anonymous 800 number can reveal a lot.
3. Thoroughly investigate all complaints and apply discipline fairly.
4. The company needs to discover the reason for the problems and attempt to solve it.
5. Be proactive about creating a content and appreciative workforce to reduce problems.
6. Focus on people first and technology second. Field more training and personal/professional development programs.
7. Teach your workforce how to deal with harassment, diversity and communication.

In addition, you can expand upon that to look at the entire work experience. Here are a baker's dozen of ways to assure that workers stay safe and that they stay happy and productive on the job.

Start at the beginning, with the hiring process. Pre-employment screenings should weed out inappropriate staff while they focus on getting the person with the right skill for the job. Drug and alcohol screening and background checks are part of this, and they can be outsourced to professionals with competencies in this area. It has been shown that pre-employment screening can significantly reduce the odds of employing a felon or rapist. When it comes to character, the past predicts the future.

In addition, drug and alcohol screening after hiring can build morale, decrease health care costs and worker's compensation claims, reduce theft and improve productivity. An internal program can also help those individuals who are found to be abusers regain mental health and become more productive employees.

Be sure to have a well-written and thorough employee manual, along with sound management training on all company policies. The manual should be clear about such mattes as bullying, sexual harassment, and the like. The manual and supervisor training should be kept updated to allow for new legislation and legal guidelines as well as new policies and procedures that reflect the latest thinking on workplace security.

Train supervisors to look for problem employees and behavioral clues, as does The Limited clothing retailer. Keep this training ongoing. There are several companies that can train people in how to deal with "hot button" issues.

Behavioral clues from workers who may "go postal" are legion, and 75% of the employees who show workplace violence will exhibit clear warning signs, so it is vital that managers know what to look for. These can include:

- Abrupt changes in behavior, such as withdrawal from family and friends. Those about to do harm distance themselves from others as they sink deeper into their own problems.
- An increased stress response concerning the workplace or personal life. Those about to act out show increasing levels of frustration.
- Inability to concentrate, as the inner demons escalate to demand more and more attention.
- Poor attendance and a decrease in productivity. Again, as rage against the employer or other workers increases,

the worker gives up on trying and instead concentrates all actions and thoughts on getting even.

- Obsessions with causes or people increase as focus on the problem or the cause of dissatisfaction becomes paramount.
- Deteriorating personal hygiene is one very obvious indication that the troubled individual has let all other considerations slip and outside influences and immaterial concerns go by the wayside in pursuit of the singular objective.
- Escalating aggressiveness, threats, or even sabotage, as the troubled worker comes closer to taking ultimate action.
- Making threats as vague or dark humor against colleagues and superiors, as the individual begins to deliver "clues" as to his eventual breakdown, perhaps as a quest for help.
- Talk of suicide can also manifest itself as the worker is torn between action and inaction.
- Flashes of real anger beginning to displace a joking this-isn't-really-serious manner.
- Reclusive or non-communicative behavior as the worker retreats further into his private thoughts and shows disdain for the rest of the world.
- Indications of alcohol or drug abuse, as the worker hopes to keep internal pain at bay with self-medication.
- Openly damaging property publicly, as anger surfaces and an end is sought.
- Bringing weapons to work, an outward display of internal stress and an indication of future action.

All of these tend to show that the worker is outwardly manifesting inward struggles, perhaps as a way of showing that he needs something he is not getting and as a signal to the outside world to provide help.

Such training is especially important in an era where employers are starting to be held liable for hiring violent employees or not heeding signs warning them of problems. In spring of 1999, two companies, Union Butterfield Corp. and Dormer Tools Inc., were found negligent of protecting workers and were made to pay almost $8 million to the families of two men killed at a tool distribution center in 1995 by a violent colleague.

The risk increases when there has been no "good-faith effort" to protect workers. And business owners and senior managers are among the most at risk population in the workplace. It is also important to know how to document any worker irregularities to create a database of information that can be used to help personnel, and protect the company from lawsuits.

Conduct a security review of the physical premises and of security procedures should trouble arise. Secure access doors at and in buildings and create and train a security staff. Again, there are outside experts that can help companies and organizations make the workplace a safe one and keep outside troubles—such as domestic violence—from becoming inside ones. A workplace with no security measures is 20 times more likely to experience a violent event.

Employers can develop more flexible work schedules. People who are torn between home and work will find that this helps them make work a part of their lives rather than the whole of it. And it will help to end the traffic congestion that makes people stressed out even before the workday begins.

Even better, when it is possible, allow people to work at home. Provide laptops, modems or other means to let them get their work done more efficiently. If it is important for workers to meet in person to discuss the work, create a core communications time when workers are expected to be on site.

Establish an internal career track to make sure workers can use all their skills and continue to learn new ones. A 1999 Emerging Workforce study showed that 21% of all workers said they planned to quit their current jobs within the next year. Over a third of these said they were dissatisfied with the firm's mentoring program, and 41% said they were insufficiently trained. Such turnover not only harms employee morale, but also contributes greatly to operating expense. Also, find ways to help workers who lack basic skills. They can be offered remedial education to help them become prepared to enter the workplace. Only 13% of companies do this now, but it is essential, and at only $289 a worker, it is not even very expensive.

Increase overall job satisfaction by involving employees more in the work and decision-making. For instance, instead of looking outside the company to find people to fit positions, make sure to solicit from inside first. Increase internal training and team-leadership opportunities. In general, let employees know they are valued and their work is appreciated. Explain it when you have to pile on work, and solicit employee opinion about problems. Stay flexible, and always look for better ways to do things, especially if you can use employee input. Ask outgoing employees why they are leaving, so you can solve any problems they can tell you about. Let the world know that you like to treat your employees well.

Create a smorgasbord of benefits, so employees can tailor benefits to their own needs. A young single worker will look at things very differently than a married person with five kids, or an older worker about to retire.

Make sure your mental health benefits are top-notch. Mental illnesses such as depression are undertreated, but not treating them is penny wise and pound foolish. Not treating mental illness costs may save some money, but it leads to increasing costs in absenteeism and unproductivity. One company found that while it saved $54 in premiums per person, the loss to business was $355 per person. A 1995 study in the "Journal of Clinical Psychiatry" found that the annual economic cost of depression, the root of many workplace violence problems, was $600 per depressed worker—one third of that for treatment and two-third for lost productivity and absenteeism.

Along the same lines, employers should establish an employee assistance program—an EAP—where employees can go to get confidential help with personal issues such as stress and mental health problems. Some of these can even help employees find day care or elder care facilities, even summer camps.

Special programs to learn to handle anger exist, so use them. Anger specialists now know that one of five people with an anger problem that is out of proportion to the stimulus have attention deficit disorder. Dr. Emil Coccaro, a professor of psychiatry at the University of Chicago School of Medicine, says that a person can have multiple small events of such anger each week in a condition he calls "intermittent explosive disorder." The school offers a treatment program for the disorder. The University of Chicago Hospitals Program on Anger Management is one of several in the country, and it is meant to help those who would throw an ashtray at colleagues, smash keyboards and shout at coworkers and it combines drug therapy with behavior modification.

Don't forget the amenities. Integra, a New York-based advisory firm, found that providing more breaks, offering juices and herbal teas instead of coffee, looking to office lighting and putting plants or fountains in place can also help. Another big help: humor. This can range from the simple Dilbert cartoon on a bulletin board to enlisting top management into silly contests to create camaraderie.

The CEO of the Brady Corporation turned things around at her company when she moved it from a company that did not allow coffee cups on the desk to one that made fun a priority. She doubled sales and almost tripled net income and market capitalization in seven years with this simple step.

Some companies are beginning to take notice of the importance of worker satisfaction. For example, United Airlines Inc. is attempting a bold new policy—a performance-based pay system. According to *BusinessWeek* magazine, this new system proved to be advantageous for the company during the recent industry labor wars. Although not all of the airline's management is thrilled about the new policy, starting in 2000, part of the compensation for top executives will be determined according to an outside survey firm that will measure UAL's worker satisfaction. The strength behind this new plan is due to UAL's unions, which own 60% of the company's shares.

Finally, encourage volunteerism in the workplace. This will give them reasons to stay motivated and connected to each other and to society. Some companies allow a few hours of paid time off if the time is spent in community service. Others make financial contributions to causes that their employees support with their time, be it a 4-H group or park clean-up program. Some cities have organizations that meet with employees to encourage volunteerism and let representatives from the company select from a full range of volunteer opportunities the ones that most interest workers at the company. This can be volunteering in nursing homes or tutoring school children.

## DEALING WITH TERRORISM

Finally, workplaces can also help workers in the short-term deal with terrorism and other tragedies by taking some additional steps. These are some ideas generated by the September 11 tragedy:

- Acknowledge worker emotions and bring sensitivity and care to work. Think about what fears workers might have about working in a high-rise building or an urban center. Take employees to lunch or let them vent in small support groups when disasters occur. Make all workers become updated on breaking news and events. Refer employees to EAPs. Trained counselors may be needed to get them back on track if untrained personnel are overwhelmed.
- Make a contribution to the cause. This can be financial, or it can mean having a blood drive, collecting food,

water, tools and clothing, helping care for children and animals, or any other positive activity.

- Reward success at work in order to give positive reinforcement and help workers think about the future and goals achieved. Allow emotional breaks that will give workers a gradual re-engagement with the work process.
- Refocus your business activity by getting people involved in small routine tasks, especially physical ones. Being able to accomplish something is cathartic. Try to get people to focus on the larger picture of what the workplace involves. Do not let the terrorists circumvent what you are trying to accomplish.

Ultimately, guidelines like this will help the workplace change to become more human. These days, futurists tell us, workers are becoming more interested in work that is involving and fulfilling, and choosing that over financial recompense. Forced out of jobs by downsizing and layoffs, they are beginning to take new career paths based on their unique skills, competencies and interests. They are tied not so much to companies or careers but to what they can apply in any field and to the many talents they have to bring to an employer. Older workers, with a wealth of experience, will achieve new prominence as enough younger workers cannot be found and as the population increases in age.

Meanwhile, workers are taking on more responsibility, and employers are learning to lead rather than manage. Time crunching and cost cutting must be met by building better relationships between organizations and their customers and clients. Workers must become more empowered, and, as reported by Roger Herman of the Herman Group in his book, *Lean and Meaningful*, they must be able to use their creativity to work smarter, not harder, doing more for customers with less internal waste of worker time, energy and skill. In short, the workplace must change to accommodate the new-style worker.

**Chapter VI**

# ROAD RAGE: ACTUALLY, I *DO* OWN THE ROAD

Road rage, the venting of anger and/or the show of power through dangerous and reckless driving, is an increasing problem with which all of us have, at one point or another, come into contact. The term was coined in 1988 and appeared in a few media stories each year until 1994, when the topic began to escalate and be perceived as an epidemic.

In fact, an American Automobile Association (AAA) survey suggests that many people think aggressive driving is a worse danger on the roads than drunk driving. It is a trigger problem because aggressive driving is a daily occurrence in every city. It can cause just as much damage and take away as many lives as driving under the influence of alcohol can.

The most recent example of road rage, one that caught the attention of the entire nation, was the story of the fluffy white dog, Leo, who was thrown into traffic and killed by Andrew Burnett. Burnett received the maximum for felony animal cruelty, a three-year prison sentence for the deed, to the applause of the courtroom and the entire country. "It's a case of age-induced violence," said the judge who did the sentencing, Kevin J. Murphy. He said that Burnett's release would pose a danger to the community.

Burnett was found after a widespread search, fueled by donated reward money. He had been jailed after that crime for the theft of a van filled with $68,000 worth of equipment from his employer, Pacific Bell. Apparently, Burnett had been involved in a similar incident of road rage five years before. Despite this, the sentencing report on the not-so-estimable Burnett has asked for probation, and his mother had called him an animal lover deserving of leniency. All of this was because of a minor fender-bender between Burnett and Leo's mistress, grieving Sara Mc Burnett. The enraged Burnett pulled the dog from his owner's lap and threw the animal into the lanes of traffic. The Burnett case tapped into a deep well of angst in the American public—the worry about road rage.

In other instances, two Washington drivers who got caught up in a screaming contest with each other lost control of their vehicles, crashing over the median into oncoming traffic and creating a four-car pileup. Three people died.

In another violent case, a Detroit man became angry with a woman in the car behind him when she accidentally bumped his car twice on a crowded bridge. So he pulled the young woman from her car, stripped her, beat her, and started to chase her. To escape another beating, she leaped over the bridge and fell 30 feet to her death.

In Colorado Springs, a 55-year-old man wanted to chastise a 17-year-old boy who had been tailgating him—so he shot him, fatally, after the boy threatened him.

In Akron, OH, a driver who felt he had been cut off by a taxi punched in the driver's side window. The frightened cabbie fought back, with a gun, shooting the man in front of his wife and four kids. They were all coming back after a July 4th fireworks display.

Road rage has even been blamed for the death of Diana, Princess of Wales in France.

Some of the lighter incidents can even seem funny—the 75-year-old in Salt Lake City that threw a bottle of prescription drugs at a man who honked at him for blocking traffic—and who then smashed the man's knees with his car. Or the attorney in the Beltway around Washington who knocked the glasses off a pregnant woman who was berating him for bumping his car into hers. Who's going to sue him?

Examples such as these are horrifying, but all too real. However, the problem is far more than these extreme examples. It can also be found in so-called normal behavior of drivers in a hurry. Loud and long honking. Cutting people off. Tailgating. Giving the finger. These are acts of aggression toward other drivers, failures to see others as fellow motorists worthy of respect and cooperation, and they are on the increase. It seems like everyone is living up to the joke on the bumper sticker: "Actually, I do own the road."

Also on the rise are behaviors that disrespect traffic laws both major and minor. A survey by the National Highway Traffic Safety Administration (NHTSA) questioned 6,000 drivers about their driving habits. While 60% of drivers surveyed feel that their safety is compromised when others speed, many of them also admit to creating safety hazards of their own. Check out these surprising numbers (based on the drivers' driving habits in the previous week):

- 30% of drivers entered an intersection while the light was red
- 26% didn't come to a complete stop at a stop sign
- 23% drove at least 10 mph over the speed limit on interstate roads
- 22% drove faster than 10 mph over the limit to "stay with the flow of traffic"
- 8% drove under the influence of alcohol
- 6% raced another driver.

Some have even seen an increase in drivers who fail to pull

over and yield the right-of-way to ambulances and fire engines, or to police cars, or drivers who do not respect the stringent laws that protect school children entering or emerging from yellow buses.

Why do drivers drive this way? Is it part of the American ideology: each of us wants our own way—now. According to the same survey, here are some reasons for bad driving habits:

- 44% of drivers speed because they are late or running behind schedule
- 12% speed just so they can keep up with the rest of the traffic
- 23% drive aggressively because they are behind schedule
- 22% do so because they are annoyed with the increased congestion of traffic
- 12% speed to pass or "teach a lesson to" careless slow or rude drivers
- 12% speed to "teach a lesson to" young and immature drivers

A report by Louis Mizell, Inc. focuses not on statistics but on the actual "reasons" some persons drive the way they do. These reasons show that many drivers have let their road rage take control, causing serious injury or even death. (All of these reasons had to be given by at least 25 different drivers to make the list):

"It was an argument over a parking space . . ."
"Nobody gives me the finger."
"The bastard kept honking and honking his horn."
"They kept tailgating me."
"He cut me off!"
"She wouldn't let me pass."
"She kept crossing lanes without signaling—maybe I overreacted but I taught her a lesson."

The hostility toward other drivers reported in the Mizell study shows that such attitudes can lead to serious results. In one reported case, a driver was shot to death "because he hit my car." A fatal crash was the result of another driver "braking and accelerating, braking and speeding up." A shooting occurred because "one motorist was playing his radio too loud." One driver accused of murder said, "He couldn't have cared less about the rest of us—he just kept blocking traffic." Another driver who was charged with attempted murder stated that the victim "practically ran me off the road. What was I supposed to do?"

A focus group conducted by the Media and Injury Prevention Program at the University of Southern California found that drivers react to frustration with aggressive acts. Just under half reported that they take dangerous steps such as breaking suddenly in front of tailgaters. One Los Angeles man said that he favored sending windshield wiper fluid over his car and onto the car behind.

In 1997, the House of Representatives addressed the issue, with hearings before its Subcommittee on Surface Transportation, chaired by Tom Petri of Wisconsin.

## WHAT CAUSES ROAD RAGE?

Clearly, too many drivers are using their cars as weapons in responding to any imaginable slight. But why are people driving with such rage?

First, there is just more traffic now to get in each other's way. In the 10 years between 1987 and 1997, the number of miles of road increased by 1%, but the mile driven jumped 35%. All that extra traffic causes congestion. The Federal Highway Administration studied 50 metropolitan areas and found that 70% of them are full at rush hour, versus only 55% in 1983. A 1996 study by the Texas Transportation Institute found that commuters in a third of the state's largest cities spend over 40 hours in traffic jams each year.

Drivers no longer head downtown during rush hours either. They head out to the suburbs, to those conglomerations and megaplexes that grew up where I-something meets up with I-something-else, and where mass transit has yet to go. So, traffic jams are broadened in scope—and in time as well, as commuting workers in office complexes head out to lunch, creating a third rush hour and more time to get on each other's nerves.

There is no longer a typical one-car family. With women working outside the home, the number of women licensed to drive increased 84% from 1970 to 1990, and the number of cars on the road more than doubled from 1970 to 1987. Cars are multiplying faster than people, it is said, and that's including the number of immigrants arriving to live here. Unlike previous immigration populations, they can no longer take the IRT subway to the Lower East Side of Manhattan.

Immigrants bring an exciting mix of cultures to this country, along with a variety of new ways to communicate with personal space, and along with new ways of driving. "There are different cultures of driving all over the world," says John Palmer, a professor in the Health Education and Safety Department at St. Cloud University in Minnesota. "If we mix these new cultures in a melting pot, what we get is a culture clash on the roadway."

Then there is the time factor. America is becoming a speedier place, and its workforce is expected to be on time and productive from the start of the workday. Hurrying drivers do not want to be thwarted in their quest to please the boss.

Plus, we can take a look at the protection offered by the car that insulates the driver. Stephanie Faul, a spokesperson for the American Automobile Association's Foundation on Traffic Safety, said, "There is something in driving which allows people to live out personalities they might not show otherwise. You feel invulnerable."

She goes on, "You're not dealing with other human beings; you're dealing with other cars. There is an anonymity to driving where the person in front of you is not a person, but a Miata or a Saturn or a Honda. And people can even respond to the make of the car itself, identifying it and personalizing it as a Yuppie-driven gas guzzling SUV or whatever. Cars too often are seen as statements rather than as transportation. At their moments of anger and frustration, people seem to forget that there are other people behind the wheels of those cars."

Many of today's cars offer size, power, a looming presence that offers support for aggressiveness and a feeling of invulnerability. Cars also offer comfort, isolation, with air conditioning and soundproofing that make drivers feel like the kings and queens of the road. The car responds to you, unlike your kids or spouse or boss or job. There is a feeling of control that is translated to a need to control over the surrounding environment as well.

John Larson, a Yale University psychiatrist, has testified that road rage lies with many drivers deducing the motivations of other drivers from the make of the car, with BMWs, pickups, sports cars and off-road vehicles seen as having aggressive personalities so that drivers respond to these unintended messages. Larson has also linked the phenomenon to sports, saying that those who wish to emulate sports heroes become "introjected" models for behavior that is demonstrated in road rage. The extreme competitiveness shown in modern society, where getting ahead, literally, is all there is, means that many drivers see driving as merely a matter of winners and losers, and we all know that nice guys finish last. "No ties," a man yells as he competes with another driver to see who will get ahead on the roadway.

Much of the problem also seems to stem from today's society, which is fueled by instant gratification. People want to be where they want to be, with minimum time getting there, and minimum hassle. *Chicago Tribune* columnist and social commentator Bob Greene has written that "road rage—and all of the other current rages—emerged because we became conditioned to having whatever we wanted at the moment we wanted it. It did not start with cars—road rage on the highways was just the ultimate result."

Expectations have been fundamentally transformed by technology, he goes on, and road rage is a result, as we bring our expectations learned from computers and the Internet to the physical road and highway. We are never to be held back or inconvenienced, and when this happens, says Greene, the result is road rage. "Speed, and the promise of it, makes us feel lazily entitled that the world be delivered in a blink, and angry when we have to wait for delivery."

Another factor may be the decline of driver's education classes. While such courses were common in the 50s and 60s, paid for by federal highway dollars, there are far fewer of them now, with only 40% of drivers completing any formal course. They vanished because a 1978 study in Georgia found that drivers who did not take the course drove as safely as those who did. So the monies went instead to seat belt and anti-drunk driving efforts. And we've all heard of how parental involvement in kid's lives has diminished. That leaves precious little in the way of resources for a 16-year-old who wants to learn how to drive. Is it another case where kids are learning life skills from peers, literally on the street? It is said that 20% to 35% of applicants fail their first driving tests.

Beyond that, Arnold Nerenberg, a clinical psychologist in Whittier, CA, who invented the term road rage and who calls himself America's Road Rage Therapist, sees the phenomenon of road rage as one aspect of humanity's evolution, noting that trying to stay ahead of others is a form of the same competitiveness. Nerenberg, who has written a book and runs a web site on the topic, counsels drivers addicted to road rage. He says that some road rage, the kind that mutters under its breath, is normal, but that aggressive rage on the road is a mental disorder and social disease that should be included in the *Diagnostic and Statistical Manual of Mental Disorders* of the American Psychiatric Association.

Others concur. It's all a matter of territoriality, they say, protecting one's turf as do the predators in the wild.

Indeed, there have been found regional variations of road rage, with a higher prevalence of impatience in the speedier East Coast than in the more laid back Midwest. A professor of psychology at Rensselaer Polytechnic in Troy, N.Y., Robert A. Barton, has conducted studies on this matter. He says: "In Boston and New York, people will honk at you before the light turns green. In Indiana, one of our researchers sat in his car at a traffic light after the light turned green. We found that the typical person . . . didn't honk for ten to fifteen seconds." Aggressive driving would seem to be contagious. One angry person takes his anger out on another. From there on, the chain of passing the anger on to others can be endless.

There is even a group of motorcyclists who travel in packs, speeding excessively and weaving in and out of highway traffic in order to incite other drivers, and to escape the police. They are so fast and facile that it generally works.

Road rage affects people even if they do not act it out in public. One Denver driver, for instance, had a 45-minute commute that left her so hostile it affected her working life for an hour after she got to work and then an hour after she got home. She had headaches, stomachaches and major problems with family and colleagues, although the other drivers never knew of her anger. This condition is probably a common one, given the increase in traffic and the frustration it can cause in the average commute.

Remember also that road rage may not be the result of something involving traffic, but it may lie with other behaviors. Even the use of a cell phone in traffic, which many believe can lead to accidents, may enrage another driver who believes that cell phones are not for drivers.

Train traffic, surprisingly, also causes road rage. Grade crossings can hold people up far longer than the time period allowed by law. They can also hold up safety vehicles such as ambulances and fire engines.

And then there's the ubiquitous orange barrel. Everywhere you go, it seems roads are being resurfaced, bridges painted, potholes filled—and drivers are held up and enraged. There appears to be increasing news about members of construction crews being killed or injured by hasty drivers. Today's hurry-up society can't seem to accommodate the slowdown, so cities everywhere are forced to post special signage reminding drivers to "Slow Down: My Daddy Works Here," or that "Fines are doubled in construction zones."

Road rage is not even necessarily something done by drivers. One bicyclist in Washington, D.C., shot the driver of a car that ran into him, and another couple of pedestrians threatened with a knife a driver who had hit their dog.

Cars are not the only weapons people use to express their rage at other drivers. There is everything from pepper spray to washer fluid to eggs. And now, with easy access to guns, aggressive driving has been known to escalate from a honk to a gunshot. Most incidences of road rage don't involve weapons, but we are beginning to see a growing number of cases in which people are fatally shot by those who can't control their anger. According to AAA, from 1990 to 1995, acts of road-related violence in the U.S. increased 51%, causing 10,037 crashes. These crashes alone were responsible for 12,610 injuries and 218 deaths.

## What Can We Do to Combat Road Rage?

We all know that road rage exists and that the problem is not one we can afford to overlook. But it might help to know that many experts feel great skepticism about the rise of road rage in America. Although they note that road rage is a problem, they feel that it is not on the rise and that reports of road rage all causing the steadily normal amount of aggressive traffic incidents are to be reassessed, and hyped, as road rage. Anecdotal evidence, the kind that leads to the idea of road rage, occurred in similar stories in the 1960s. The AAA study was not scientifically conducted; rather, it was compiled from news reports and insurance claims in 16 cities.

Indeed, the NHTSA's administrator, Ricardo Martinez, has gone on record that "one-third of traffic crashes and two-thirds of resulting fatalities can be attributed to behavior associated with aggressive driving." But it is important to interpret this by knowing that the term "associated with" includes any manner of activities such as changing lanes without signaling and driving on the shoulder. Road rage has been used to describe such activities as a protest against building a highway near a historic monument or anger at high insurance premiums.

When it comes to actual statistics, the AAA study found just a few incidents—218 of traffic fatalities directly the result of enraged driving, in a period when 290,000 people died in traffic accidents. And of 20 million injured drivers, only just over 12,000 were caused by angry motorists—a fairly small percentage. The *Atlantic Monthly* reported that there is little statistical evidence that there is more aggressive driving in this country. It did, however, point out that there is an epidemic in the running of red lights, an increase of 14% between 1992 and 1996, according to the Department of Transportation.

However, no matter what the trend in road rage is, no matter how many or how few incidents are, it is important to prevent as many as possible.

## CALMING INDIVIDUAL DRIVERS

In whatever quantities, road rage—and terrible tales such as that of Leo the dog—exists. Even if the stats are in your favor, in the end it can come down to just you and the other angry guy on the road. The question is: What can we do about it? Road rage can be controlled and prevented, if, on an individual basis, people can learn to recognize their emotions and to control them.

Although feelings such as fatigue, anger, depression, annoyance, illness, and inattention may be unavoidable, drivers don't have to get behind the wheel when they feel that way. If worse comes to worse, take a cab, ride the bus, enjoy the many forms of public transportation. It may save your life . . . or those of others.

But if a person does need to drive, here are some suggestions from the experts on keeping cool in traffic:

1. Count to 10. Counting to ten will calm you down enough to lower your level of adrenaline, which will help you breathe easier and relax.
2. Plan your trips wisely. If you know you have a problem with road rage, arrange your trip to avoid rush hour and other heavy-traffic situations.
3. Give yourself a little extra time even just a few minutes— so you won't feel rushed.
4. Avoid dangerous behaviors, like tailgating, blocking the passing lane, changing lanes without signaling, parking across two or more parking spaces.
5. Play music you enjoy or sing to yourself in the car. Listen to a taped book. Give yourself a pep talk about honor and decency—anything to lift your spirits. Soothing or classical music could work better than rap. Be silly— laughter helps.
6. Make sure your seat is comfortable and that the temperature is right. You don't need anything else making you feel hotheaded.
7. Remember that drivers are a community, and that driving is truly a communal activity in which people perform better when they are following the rules and working together.
8. If you feel rage even before you get into the car, give yourself some time to calm down first. It is better to be a minute or two late than to be the cause of a wreck. Remember that anger harms your body and that humor can diffuse anger.
9. Get counseling. Jerry Deffenbacher, Ph.D., a psychology professor at Colorado State University, has studied anger and road rage for two decades, and he has used relaxation

and cognitive relations therapy for the condition. The therapy involved relaxation techniques, such as tensing and releasing muscles, deep breathing, visualizing rage situations with a therapist, and working on anger-provoking thought processes. Both reduce the intensity and frequency of anger.

## DEALING WITH THE OTHER GUY

To protect yourself from other motorists who may react with road rage to what you are doing, it is important to follow these simple rules:

1.  Do not respond to problems with an angry gesture or action. If you have an encounter with an aggressive driver, let him pass at the first opportunity. Avoid confrontation and eye contact with dangerous drivers.
2.  Understand that it is not your job to teach anyone else how to drive. If you have a problem with an unsafe or reckless driver, let the authorities handle it. Get to a phone and notify them yourself if it will make you feel better. Or carry a cell phone, pull over safely and use it. Just don't take the law into your own hands.
3.  Pretend the other drivers are people you know and that you will see them at a party later. We are all more understanding when we know the persons involved in a problem. Think to yourself: "He must just be having a bad day." One incident of road rage in highway-crazy Los Angeles was thwarted when the participants realized they were neighbors. Also know that what happens in traffic may not be personal. The guy who cuts you off may not have seen you or may not be local and aware of the road and so need to make changes suddenly.
4.  Stay away from erratic drivers. If you have an incidence involving a driver who is enraged, stay in the car and do not expose yourself to trouble. Remain calm.

5. Give way to people getting on highways in front of you.
6. One key factor in reversing road rage in others is to apologize. Over 85% of the enraged say that they would drop the matter if the other driver were to apologize and to indicate some concern over what happened. In this way, the other driver would not need to teach him or her a "lesson." Some suggest that there be developed a universal "sorry" hand signal drivers can use, such as holding the back of the hand to the slightly bowed forehead.

Others suggest that drivers make a large print SORRY sign about 10 inches by 4 inches and keep it on a map holder or sun visor. At night, drivers can illuminate the sign using the car's ceiling light. Drivers have been known to smile when they see such signs.

Some even advocate beginning a public road rage prevention campaign using such signs, which could be distributed by radio station sponsors with their logos on them.

## SOCIETAL SITUATIONS

Other suggestions to combat road rage are designed to reach society as a whole instead of the individual on the road.

Some advocate that we teach road rage prevention in health classes, or in one of the few driver's education classes that is left. It's easy to get a license in this country, and young drivers, those who have the least control over their emotions and the least experience, are more likely to be killed in car crashes than for any other reason. But there is some indication that drivers' education is on the way back. Michigan, Maryland, Oregon and California have seen teen accident rates drop as they began to offer higher levels of driving privileges to those who complete such courses. And in the latter state, traffic offenders attend driving classes led by comics who offer such programs as Traffic School for Chocoholics.

The Maryland Highway Department is running a campaign called The End of the Road for aggressive drivers. Among other things, it uses electronic billboards to flash calming messages.

Some states, such as Delaware, Pennsylvania and New Jersey, use special highway patrols to target aggressive drivers. And Ohio uses its aviation group to report aggression to its road patrol cars, which by law must be marked. The operation, called TRIAD for Targeting Reckless, Intimidating and Aggressive Drivers, let state troopers join forces with local law enforcement and resulted in more than 3,000 citations.

Cities such as San Francisco are installing cameras at stop lights to catch offenders by photographing their license plates. The number of drivers who ran lights in the City by the Bay dropped by 42%.

In Hawaii, one university professor suggested that we begin to emphasize "supportive driving" rather than defensive driving, where the other driver is regarded as the enemy. Traffic is, after all, a cooperative venture. Watch drivers at a four-way stop sometimes handle motions that are almost ballistic. In fact, Whittier's Dr. Nerenberg offers an 18-page booklet called *Overcoming Road Rage* that concentrates on 10 steps of compassion and stresses that the other guy is a human being as well.

Finally, realize that no matter how individuals operate, overall, traffic is becoming safer thanks to legislative efforts such as the rise in the drinking age, seat belt laws and lower speed limits, as well as better traffic engineering and technological advances such as anti-locking brakes and high-mounted brake lights. Keep your car in good operating condition, and get behind efforts to improve the use of seat belts and reduce drunk driving.

## Chapter VII

# AIR RAGE:
# FLYING THE UNFRIENDLY SKIES

At one time, flying was an adventure. People dressed up for it. Of course, that was in the days when air travel was a comparatively rare phenomenon, not a democratic exercise. Today, people getting onto airplanes tend to dress down and even to the point of wearing combat fatigues. And there may be a reason for this, if a quick look at some recent headlines about air travel has any lessons to offer.

For instance, on a flight from South Africa to London, a drunken plumber insisted that he be allowed to view graphic pornography. The crew's refusal to let him do so led him to swear at the attendants, threaten them with death, and attack the six crew members who were trying to restrain him. Three of these were injured. A physician passenger was required to sedate and monitor him. Damage to the plane was estimated at $10,000. The man, intoxicated while on the ground, had been hallmarked as trouble by the ground crew.

A banker from Greenwich, Connecticut, flying From South

America to New York, assaulted a flight attendant and defecated on a food cart.

Three siblings flying alone for the first time to their grandmother's home in Atlantic City were overwhelmed by a passenger behind them who berated and swore at them for moving around. The woman kicked their seatback so hard that it collapsed on one of the kids and pinned him down. The woman threatened to kill them and sue their parents. The parents, however, are doing the suing.

This is air rage, and it's been making headlines in unprecedented numbers. But it's not just the passengers who are under attack. Flight attendants seem to bear the brunt of the problem. In a confined environment miles removed from help, there is no way to walk away or get help.

A flight attendant for USAirways was beaten by a psychotic passenger, losing 2 ½ years of her work life and wages, in addition to needing shoulder and knee surgery and psychological counseling.

Another passenger broke into the cockpit of a San Francisco-bound plane and threatened to kill the crew as he tried to take over the controls. He was restrained until the plane landed.

One passenger threw a can of beer at an attendant and bit a pilot, sending the Continental flight back to Anchorage. In another instance, a drunken old lady punched one flight attendant.

Trouble also comes to those who stay on the ground. Ground crews, who are represented by the International Association of Machinists and Aerospace Workers, say that although air rage is a common concern, ground rage is equally scary. One member of the ground crew of one airline was confronted by a passenger and suffered a broken neck. Another had his nose broken. A third was picked up and thrown against a wall. Ground crews are often sworn at and have been known to have luggage thrown at them. In one incident in Detroit, holiday decorations at the ticketing desk became projectiles as angry passengers hurled them at agents. Unfortunately, one of the biggest problems is that ground crews are not kept up to date, and so cannot pass on vital and correct information to frantic, hostile passengers.

The International Transport Workers' Federation (ITWF), an umbrella group representing several unions, such as those of flight attendants and ground crews, has said that air rage incidents such as these have increased from 1,232 in 1994 to 5,416 in 1997. Some 310 unruly passenger incidents were reported to the Federal Aviation Administration in 1999.

Anecdotally, the number of incidents and their severity seems to be going up as well, says Dawn Deeks, a spokeswoman for the Association of Flight Attendants (AFA), which represents the flight attendants at 27 airlines. The Air Transport Association pegs the number of incidents at 4,000 a year. The official number can vary because of different definitions and reporting strategies. Says the AFA, "There are no reliable industry-wide numbers on air rage. The FAA only reports the number of enforcement actions it takes, since airlines are not required to report air rage incidents."

Air rage has been defined by the ITWF as "interfering with crew members in the performance of their duties," but it also includes actions taken against other passengers. These incidents can range from noise and disturbing the peace to actual violence that threatens the lives of passengers and crew in the vulnerable sky craft. The AFA categorizes them into alcohol-related incidents, the use of prohibited electronic devices, smoking in lavatories, drug-related incidents, including medicines, and bomb or hijack threats. But all represent a rent in the social fabric that asks for reasonable public behavior for the good of all.

The AFA says that one study shows that unruly passengers can disrupt pilots and cause serious flying errors. In 40% of the 152 cases studied, pilots had to leave the cockpit or were interrupted in their flight routine. In a quarter of those cases, this led to errors such as too much speed, flying at the wrong altitude or taxiing across the wrong runway. Problems also result in emergency landings, cockpit break-ins, physical injury and emotional trauma.

## WHAT'S THE PROBLEM?

The problem, really, is that more people than ever are able to fly. It's more democratic than it's ever been, with fares remarkably low. It's really a success story, as deregulation created the low fares and abundance of opportunity for everyone to enjoy an activity that used to be reserved for the wealthy. In 1977, 250 million people flew. The number is estimated to be over a billion in 2010. And don't forget that airplanes also carry cargo and other goods.

But that rapid growth created by deregulation has caused problems big and small as growing numbers of passengers swamped an antiquated system. They include long lines for tickets and boarding, uncertain and arbitrary fares, flights that are either delayed or cancelled, with absolutely no information given about what's going on, no apologies or explanations, no compensation, overcrowded planes and overbooked flights that get you bumped, missed connections with little help making new ones or getting food or lodging vouchers.

Then there are labor problems and strikes, grouchy, rude service, cutbacks on service personnel, bad food and not enough of it, either peanuts on the flight or not being able to get peanuts because some kid just might eat one, lousy in-flight movies, unhealthy, germ-laden air, small overheads or delays while passengers ahead of you get squared away with everything they own, conflicting carrier policies, lost baggage, tiny seats with no leg room, planes upon which you hurry to board on, yet still, you end up sitting and sitting on the runway with no takeoff, no food service, no bathrooms. Enough for you?

In short, it is often a lot of little things that add up to one big one. A short delay is announced. OK, fine. But that is added to with another 20-minute delay, followed by another and then another. All with no explanation. Or if there is one, it is said to be weather-related, but then it mysteriously changes to a mechanical problem. A government study has found that on trips of 500 miles or less, travel by car is as fast or faster than air travel, door to door. And in a car, you know where you are and have more control over things.

In general, the problem with flying these days would be enough to try the patience of a saint, which few of us are. It came strongly to public attention when that plane full of passengers sat on the tarmac in Detroit in a snowstorm for eight hours, with overflowing toilets—and a terminal with all the amenities just feet away. A cell phone call to the airline president was needed to get relief.

Business travelers often leave a day early and add food and a hotel bill to the cost of doing business, along with time they lose away from the office and from their families—just to be sure not to miss important meetings. This, of course, adds to the other stressors in their lives. For instance, one 27-year-old marketing executive left home the night before an important meeting to take the short hop from New York to Washington— and it took him 16 sleepless hour to get there by way of St. Louis, Charlotte, and Baltimore, due to delayed, cancelled and overbooked flights. Despite his caution, he was late for his meeting.

This kind of service has made business travelers leery. One exec, tired of sitting on runways and losing luggage, bought a share in a corporate aircraft fleet that gets him there on time, even at a much greater expense. But recent cutbacks in business travel due to stock market worries are forcing many business travelers onto the most economical, yet problematic flights: those with numerous stops that are just made to create arrival delays.

A *Newsweek* poll said that 57% of travelers it surveyed say flying has gotten worse in the last five years. When asked what the biggest problem with flying was, 29% said flight delays were the biggest problem and 27% claimed it was cramped quarters on the aircraft. However, says *Newsweek*, 69% of the passengers surveyed were not willing to spend more on fares to fix these problems.

These perceptions are backed up by statistics. The Department of Transportation says that over 23% of flights departed late in 2000, about 3.25% were canceled and over 27% arrived late. The airlines say that 70% of all delays are weather related. Overall, in the year 2000, one in four planes was delayed or cancelled, costing at least $5 billion a year at a conservative estimate. This is especially upsetting when you know that if a plane leaves the gate within 15 minutes of its departure time but then sits on the runway for hours, it's considered on time. And the number of grounded passengers is said to have risen by 400% in the last five years.

Also, airlines are forced to overbook flights because some 10% to 15% of passengers do not show up. But when they do, and people are bumped off of flights they think they were to make, anger ensues. Overbooking, on the other hand, was said to be up 50% in the first quarter of 1999.

On-time stats are usually kept and reported by citing the performance of specific airlines, but a 2001 release by the Department of Transportation showed some interesting statistics broken down by airport. It found that cloudy Seattle and busy New York topped the list of late arrivals, with 31.3% late in the first part of the year, followed by 31.1% at LaGuardia. Three of every 10 flights were late into Los Angeles, and a quarter of all flights were late, and that means by 15 minutes at Boston, JFK in New York, San Francisco, O'Hare, Philly, Phoenix, San Diego and Newark. For the larger period of the year 2000, 43% of aircraft arriving LaGuardia were late, but this number dropped when a lottery was used to award landing slots, reducing the number of flights.

Late flights have a boomerang effect as passengers arrive too late to meet connection and as they struggle up crowded aisles with baggage they are afraid to check—delaying plane loading substantially.

No wonder there is air rage. But who is at fault for all of this? Everyone blames everyone else. Airlines blame the weather and air traffic controllers, controllers blame airlines that overburden the system, passengers blame attendants, attendants blame passengers. But the problems are largely systemic.

First, there are a lot of airplanes in the sky. America represents one third of the world aviation market, and a fleet of over 7000 planes makes 8 million scheduled commercial flights each year, or over 22,000 a day, and these planes carry over 600 million passengers. This means there is a literal shortage of runways to allow all of the takeoffs that are needed into and landings from the congested skies. Only two major hubs, Denver and Dallas/Fort Worth, have been built since jet service began 40 years ago. The top 30 busiest airports handle over 70% of all air traffic but have only opened six new runways in the last 10 years between them. New airports and expanded runways at existing airports are fought by neighbors and environmentalists, and even if wanted, they can be held up for years by overwhelming amounts of regulatory paperwork.

The five biggest airports in the country, LaGuardia, O'Hare, Newark, Atlanta and San Francisco, accounted for 200,000 delays, and LaGuardia alone accounted for 20% of all the nation's delays.

It seems that all flights hope to leave in the same two windows of rush hour, early in the morning or the late afternoon, with the smaller, slower planes taking up an overwhelming amount of time per passenger served. And airlines try to get as many flights as they can into this window, creating an impossible situation for the controllers. Flight times become increasingly unrealistic, good for selling tickets but very bad for pleasing customers with on-time service.

Air traffic controllers are also working with outdated technologies and with outdated procedures based on models from decades ago. In 1999, they scratched more than 10% of the commercial flights in the U.S.

There are also psychological factors at work. Unlike car

travel, in the air, the traveler is not in control and is at the mercy of a number of unseen elements. He or she is usually in the dark about where problems occur and when they can be rectified. The weather, congestion in other cities and a down traffic system are all blamed on the airline.

Indeed, much of the problem with air rage is caused by an act of God or the weather. No one can do anything about it, and it can create havoc in the air and in the airport, as travelers are stranded for hours or days because of something no one can control. It may not even be local—it's disconcerting to see a sunny sky outside and know your plane can't take off because of turbulence on the route or heavy fog at O'Hare. Perhaps worst of all, weather is not just an annoyance. It can be positively dangerous to the flyer. And it's all out of our control, the most frustrating thing imaginable.

Travel is also just a stressful time in general, because it involves meeting deadlines and being time conscious. It is also a very public activity when it takes place on an airline, unlike in a car. At all times, the air traveler is subject to the scrutiny of others.

Airplanes, like ships, are not democratic institutions. They have captains and crew who are in charge for very legitimate safety reasons, but this can bother the psyches of individuals who need to be "in charge" at all times. And this goes double for the kind of people who demand special attention because they have paid a lot. They are used to knowing that money talks, but on a plane, safety is paramount.

Flying is also just intrinsically scary and aircraft seem to be very vulnerable objects. Flying involves something seemingly against nature, taking a big heavy object into the air and making it stay there. Many people have a fear of flying to a large or small extent, and there is an undercurrent of anxiety despite the airlines' safety record that leads to unrest and to a need to feel secure and even cosseted.

Indeed, many fliers turn to alcohol to reduce the anxiety of flight, and in many cases of air rage, alcohol is a major contributing factor. The Association of Flight Attendants executive William Lehman says that passengers drinking too much is just a recipe for a bad flight. Many of the anecdotes at the top of this chapter were fueled by passengers who had had too much to drink. Some passengers may take a nip or two to ward off fear, others use the stuff as a celebratory or enjoyable substance to make the flight more special, and far too many come on with a deliberate attitude already three sheets to the wind.

Lack of oxygen is also a causative factor in air rage. Like alcohol, it causes people to become belligerent.

Health matters can also be a concern. This can be a major matter, as when cramped seating means a risk of deep vein thrombosis on long flights, so that blood clots can occur—a 28-year-old British woman died from DVT after a 20-hour flight last year from Australia. Or it can just be the frustration and worry that arises from sitting in uncirculated, dry air that is too hot or too cold and full of germs. Feelings of being in an unhealthy environment do not lead anyone to calmness of spirit. The AFA notes that Congress is looking at a bill that would require airlines to record and respond to cabin air quality complaints about contaminated cabin air.

## WAYS TO OVERCOME OR REDUCE AIR RAGE

Reducing air rage and making the skies a friendlier place will take a variety of actions, both on a personal level and on a systemic level. Since all players have a part in creating air rage, we—airlines, passengers, government and crews—must all play a part in fixing it. And many have already begun to do so.

Congress has passed a law allowing the FAA to fine unruly passengers up to $25,000 per violation, up from $1,100 and to allow federal officials to deputize local law officers to arrest or detain troublemakers, which in many cases they could not do before. Disrupting a flight can mean a 20-year sentence and $250,000 fine. Tougher laws will help. However, the AFA says the FAA has issued only 18 fines in a year, and has collected only one of these. The deputizing of local law enforcement is spotty, with jurisdictional confusion on international flights.

The overall air industry can begin flying in free flight patterns rather than fixed lanes, guided by new GPS technology, allowing more planes to be in the air and more passengers to be served more quickly. And the air traffic control system can be updated with new technologies and a coordinated approach that will make it more efficient and less disruptive, reducing delays and cancellations. Some suggest commercializing it to allow for an investment in new technology that would quickly recap itself.

The air industry must work to reduce congestion by building new airports and runways and coordinate the various regulatory agencies to improve development times for this new infrastructure. The rest of society could be building new high speed railroads between major population centers to help people on those shorter, under 500-mile hops.

Airports can add amenities that let passengers pass waiting time pleasantly and work off steam beyond sitting in a bar and fueling air rage. In Las Vegas, there's a 24-hour fitness center near the baggage claim for a moderate fee, with workout clothes and shoes available. At Dallas-Fort Worth, there is a golf course that rents clubs to bored passengers, while shuttles take them to a mall for shopping, movies and ice skating. San Francisco invited the fog-bound into first-class restaurants. Austin has free concerts on Friday evenings. Denver offers musicians strolling from gate to gate as well as caricature artists. Right across from the United gates in Pittsburgh is a massage therapist who'd like the airlines to offer vouchers for his services. Minneapolis and six other cities offer DVD and player rentals through InMotion Pictures, a Jacksonville, FL-based entrepreneur. Passengers can view it there, or take it with them on the trip, along with other movies.

Policy changes are also needed. Airlines can also adopt and enforce written policies on disruptive passengers that spell out steps to be taken and train attendants on standard ways to deal with unruly passengers. For instance, USAirways distributes a handbook on how to deal with problem passengers and provides plastic restraints for use if needed. Crew training also includes how to manage disruptive passengers.

There is also a need to make incidence reports standard, say crews, and mandatory, in order to track the scope of the problem.

Passengers must become educated about their responsibilities and the penalties for crew interference through written materials and announcements during the pre-flight passenger briefing.

Airlines must also keep passengers better informed about what is happening with weather or delays or whatever and help them to make connections to the next airport. Most of the problem with air rage is that fliers are being kept in the dark about what is going on, what causes flight problems and when they would be resolved.

Delta was praised for doing just this when it began rewarding employees for keeping customers aware of why delays occurred or what would be happening, while America West instituted a customer advocate at each airport. Even better, airlines must begin actually helping customers with problems rather than just informing them that they were occurring.

Airlines should make ticket purchases and other rule-laden procedures faster and simpler. Anger arises when the airline is difficult to deal with and things seem arbitrary, changeable and mysterious. Airlines sometimes seem to exist to make flying harder instead of easier, a cardinal rule of customer service. Some are addressing the problem. United, for instance, is investing $150 million to cut waiting times at airports by using electronic kiosks to issue boarding passes and assign seats.

Passengers should prepare for flights by determining how best to interact with fellow passengers in seats next to you and around you. Open channels of communications, and prepare also to bring a book or music to get through the long hours. If problems occur, just walk away, and be sure to alert the crew if you see signs of a problem.

Airlines must make bigger seating areas with more legroom for all passengers, as American did recently, and bigger areas for overhead storage, as Continental has done. Crowded seating is regarded as one of passengers' biggest rage producers, and it's unhealthy as well.

However, it is important for passengers to know that deep vein thrombosis can affect anyone, be he in the cramped economy class seats or in the first class section. The important thing for the vulnerable population is not to sit still for too long, but to move about as much as possible.

Because intoxication is a major cause of air problems, passengers should limit their drinking and remember to follow the rules of polite behavior rather than relying on a sense of entitlement that may not be able to be followed in the confines of the cabin. Airlines should act to make sure that there are no drunks allowed to board. Ground crew must be empowered to regulate this, said the AFA president Patricia Friend. Again, more training is needed here, and free drinks should not be allowed as compensation for problems. In the meantime, Sen. Dianne Feinstein has suggested there be a law enforcing a two-drink maximum on flights.

Passengers should be agreeable to paying more if they want better service and to purchasing tickets based on service rather then frequent flier miles. On the other hand, if money is precious, lower your expectations on comfort and allow more time for travel. Today's passengers pay 70 cents less per each passenger mile, when adjusted for inflation, than they did 20 years ago.

Passengers could also try to use secondary airports that may cost less and reduce congestion. In general, remember that you get what you pay for. They could also be more careful about following rules for on-board luggage, carrying on only small, easily stowable rather than blocking aisles during the boarding procedure.

Since the sky workers are even more at risk from air rage

than passengers, it is not surprising that they are in the forefront of doing something about it. Flight attendants have asked the nations of the world to create a convention that would ensure prosecution of offenders as well as for airlines to provide training and restraint equipment, as well as better security policies.

The International Association of Machinists and Aerospace Workers holds an annual day of action against air rage, Global Zero Air Rage Day, with conferences and informational picketing on the topic. The Association of Flight Attendants members blanket air travelers with leaflets on air rage during a day each year that is devoted to air safety. They seek written policies on how to deal with incidents, better attendant training in how to deal with crises, better security and the availability of restraints, as well as an overall reporting system. They also advocate better passenger education about laws governing interference with crew and warnings about the consequences of air rage.

In addition, flight attendant Renee Sheffer and her husband Mike has begun a nonprofit organization called Skyrage, meant to increase awareness of air rage, support its victims and learn to prevent it. Sheffer, a victim of air rage, has a Web site, *www.skyrage.org*, that tells more.

**Chapter VII**

# RAGE AGAINST THE GOVERNMENT: TERRORISM

Our world is being threatened by terrorism. Be they international regimes sending out terrorist thugs or homegrown militias, they have one common goal: to prove that our country is no longer protected by its government. And if the government can't protect us, what good will it be for our country?

Terrorists want to show us that our government is vulnerable, that it is not prepared to take care of us in the face of a disaster. They want us to believe that our police cannot take control of riots, that youth gangs are able to destroy entire neighborhoods without any retaliation, that cities can be looted in the wake of such disasters as hurricanes and tornadoes.

They want us to see that we are the victims, that we are not protected. Therefore, because our country is "going to hell in a hand basket," maybe we should all either join up with them—a group of people who really care, who will provide us with the protection we need, if they are domestic terrorists—or throw in the towel and let their group have its own way in the world, if they are foreign.

This is what they want us to think. If we roll out the welcome mat, the terrorists can step in and take over . . . and they believe we will welcome their arrival. Frightening and killing people seems to be the way these groups are preparing to make themselves welcome. Our fears are coming true as we now suspect at least ten countries are developing biological weapons . . . weapons that could be even more deadly than nuclear and chemical weapons at a fraction of the cost.

Incidents are designed to be brutal, bloody and worthy of an appearance on the TV with film at 11. We see it in the news every day—the latest act of violence, be it against a group of people or an innocent child. More and more, we witness the effects of violent acts of terrorism at places we often go—places where we should feel safe, such as school and work, or even church. So where can we feel safe? What can we do to prevent such acts of terrorism?

Of course, since September 11, 2001, none of this is news. I will discuss that specific case later on, but first I'd like take a look at terrorism, its psychology and sociology, as a background.

# A GLOBAL LOOK

When asked, the average person will probably think of terrorism as an international problem, the result of activities by foreigners across the seas that are bent on some political agenda or another in some third world country. We have reason to believe that many foreign states and countries are fielding terrorist enterprises. They are legion, with agendas, weaponry and procedures as varied as the places they represent: Asia, South America, Europe, the Middle East, Africa. Everywhere, it seems, but Antarctica. But give it time.

The FBI defines terrorism as the "unlawful use of force or violence against persons or property to intimidate or coerce a government, the civilian population or any segment thereof in furtherance of political or social objectives." Sounds pretty mechanical, doesn't it? What is not mentioned in this definition is that occasions of terrorism aren't limited to foreign countries that are suffering from political unrest. It can (and does) happen everywhere, and often occurs on a daily basis, even in this country. For this reason, it is not surprising that many people, even in developed, democratic and stable countries, live in constant fear of being the victim of a terrorist attack in their daily lives.

Acts of terrorism ranged from the Flight 103 disaster in 1988 when a plane crashed in Lockerbie, Scotland, after terrorist sabotage by two Libyans to the recent horrifying actions by Osama bin Laden's Al-Qaida. The memories are terrifying.

The Library of Congress has, in the wake of September 11, posted on its web site, (www.loc.org/rr/frd/) a research article on the sociology and psychology of terrorism. It's worth reading. It talks about who becomes a terrorist and why. Before, says the report, terrorists wanted a lot of people watching, not a lot dead. That idea was based on a supposition that terrorism was normative, says the report, and that using weapons of mass destruction, WMD, would alienate the terrorists' supportive constituency.

That is true of secular terrorists like the IRA. But when religious terrorists such as Osama bin Laden are considered, the equation differs. The trend in terrorism, says the report, is on religious extremists who wish to maximize the violence and whose enemy is the rest of the world, not just a perceived secular political oppressor. Because of this, the report says, the groups' primary satisfaction is not so much taking credit for attacks as the private happiness that it caused the attack and resulting suffering.

Thus, the report cites religious terrorists as the most dangerous as they hope to emulate God, or their concept of Him.

A Canadian newspaper reminded its readers that Americans were the first to help Europe recover from World War II with the Marshall Plan and Truman Policy, and that it helped Japan as well, forgave war debts, propped up the French government in 1956, and sent aid to earthquake victims across the world. He reminded readers that our technology put a man on the moon, that we rebuilt railways in France, Germany and India, that we are open to the public even in our scandals. Yet until September 11, 2001, few countries repaid us in either money or in respect. Now, we can begin to see that changing.

## THE DOMESTIC FRONT

But Americans are worried about terrorism on the home front as well. The attack on the World Trade Centers in 1993 proved that foreign terrorists can and do get into this country quite easily and can approach almost any target with the intent of doing great harm.

One fear is that these terrorists may obtain chemical, nuclear, and biological weapons. The bio-weapon, a "poor man's bomb," is potentially deadlier than a nuclear device or chemical weapon. These can include such horrors as agri-terrorism, unleashing a disease like smallpox, or smuggling in some cells that would create our own domestic version of mad cow disease right here in the United States. Rumors tell us that at least 10 other countries are developing bio-weapons.

However, to be awake and aware is to realize that much of the terrorism we experience and fear is now the product of Americans on American soil, and that the weapons can include good old American guns and fertilizer bombs. Who can forget the words, and the images? An Oklahoma City government building with a multi-story, Godzilla-like bite taken out of it. A weary firefighter carrying a dead toddler just taken from a day care center. Teddy bears tied to a fence. And a memorial with chairs and a clock stopped at 9:02.

Or a madman trying to recreate a smiley face in mailbox bombings over the map of the U.S. Or five persons who died from anthrax mailed in letters to two members of Congress, and a world turned upside down.

And there are words like Waco, Ruby Ridge, the New World Order that symbolize the militia movement in the United States and its extreme distrust of government. For example, in our country alone, there are an estimated 800 organizations operating in the new "Patriot Movement," and its membership is still continuing to grow.

These are armed militias who desire to overthrow our government and control our nation themselves. More than 440 of these terrorist groups are armed, and they are active in every state. There are familiar old names like the Ku Klux Klan and new ones. And it has been documented that the smaller groups are consolidating and joining with the larger ones, giving them more power and prestige.

In addition, the Senate Judiciary Committee has identified at least 250 militias as posing "a moderate to strong risk to local law enforcement." They used to target individual police officers, talk show hosts they did not like and informers. But they are also changing their strategies, and now are accepting damage to collateral damage like the little kids in day care centers in Oklahoma City. All of these have access to the same methodologies that society does: computer and cable abilities to tell the world of their sorrow and their beliefs.

Those beliefs are becoming blended, so that right wingers and the left can join forces to target globalism or promote animal rights and environmentalism. Hate groups are consolidating into larger ones and reaching out from the fringe to enlist the mainstream.

Others with a vengeance against government are those who start riots in the inner city, or youth gangs who begin insurrections to show their power and perhaps grab a few consumer goods. Sometimes, these riots are in direct response to a government action, such as a jury verdict with which they disagree. Who can forget what happened after the Rodney King verdict?

In the spring of 1992, in the wake of a trial exonerating white police officers in the videotaped and televised beating of

Rodney King, the city of Los Angeles went on a riot that resulted in the savage beating of Reginald Denny, a truck driver who just happened to be in the area. Fires were torched several miles apart, rather than in a concentrated area, as during the Watts riots in the 1960s. Snipers kept the fire department from responding as the jobs and futures of those who lived in the area went up in flame.

But this kind of rage is not over. It is as recent as last year in Cincinnati, when Timothy Thomas, a man wanted on 14 various criminal counts, led cops through the back alleys on a chase through a tough neighborhood and only then turned to reach for something in his waistband that was not a gun, but which the policeman who shot him guessed wrongly that it would be. And so the riot.

## WHY IS IT HAPPENING?

Riots are the effects of rage and frustration with government action. Unfortunately, the prevalence of unfair judicial treatment in the past, dating from the Reconstruction Era and proceeding through the time of lynchings and Jim Crow laws has led to a lack of confidence by blacks in the U. S. justice system. The National Center for State Courts shows that 68% of black people believe that "people like them" are discriminated against in court, while only 33% of Hispanics thought so. Note the differing opinions by black and by white Americans about the decision in the O.J. Simpson trial.

In inner city riots sparked by police actions or judicial decisions, rioters blame white racism, the fact that we have two nations, deparate and unequal, and that they suffer a form of economic discrimination. But 72% of those indicted for riot-related cries were already criminals. Among the buildings torched in that Cincinnati riot was an anti-poverty agency offering job training and financial help. Riots—irrational, unplanned and notoriously unproductive—in fact, harm most of all the local people who have to live with burned out buildings and lack of retailers willing to open there.

Rioters decried the 15 black men shot by police, but four of the shootings were done by black officers, and only two of the total 15 shootings were thought to be worth investigating, as the rest were of very dangerous men caught in criminal acts. Many Cincinnati leaders in the community spoke out against rioters and for hard work, committed families and a moral stance.

One reason for political terrorism, both domestic and foreign, is that traditional borders are disappearing and new borders are emerging. These changes have brought about violent cycles of war, poverty, famine, and refugees. The world's population is fluid, and restless. There is, therefore, an increasing competition for jobs and resources. In many cases, because of the horrible problems in their homelands, people flee to the United States, some illegally. Some even commit fraud to get here.

Some immigrants are so eager to get here they take their lives in their hands. They go to the sea in small, ramshackle boats, often dying in the process, as they try to escape Cuba or Haiti for what they hope will be a better life. Elian Gonzales is a poster child for this movement.

Others trust themselves to "coyotes," men who promise to bring them to America in enclosed trucks for high fees, but who often abandon them to die on the way after getting their only object, the money.

In other parts of the world, women and young girls desperate to make a better life for themselves contract with agents who promise factory, hotel or waitress work across one border or another only to find themselves trapped in a far different and more demeaning, and inescapable, profession.

Our border with Mexico is an example. It barely exists, despite U.S. Army attempts to build walls to keep illegal immigrants out. Despite this, however, in San Diego, road signs are a common sight that warn of "immigrant crossings," much like those that signal deer or duck crossings up north. The media have reported what is happening by describing the mixed culture that is developing, with American companies and Mexican workers both creating a common culture.

In short, due to technology that makes both travel and the exchange of information easier, the world is getting smaller. Without a doubt, though, whatever develops in the way of immigration and the growing diversity of cultures, there will be those who will think it is wrong and will rise up in terrorism against it. Other government actions and social movements are equally upsetting to some terrorist groups.

*Guns.* There are many reasons that these domestic extremist groups, along with their foreign counterparts, have made the government their enemy.

One of these is gun control efforts. Membership in "patriot" and other antigovernment organizations is reportedly growing, spurred by a reaction against the 1993 Brady Bill and other recently enacted gun control legislation. This is the kind of legislation that these groups see as making the local, state and national governments their enemy. Former FBI chief Louis Freeh states that patriot organization members, suspicious of government, often stockpile munitions in anticipation of a future standoff with federal, state and/or local law enforcement agents. They are seriously afraid of having their guns taken, and in this case, a major cause for which they fight also becomes a major weapon.

*Patriotism.* Another reason may be even more surprising: patriotism. The foreign terrorists are motivated by a love for their own particular country, region, leader or political movement. And the United States may be working directly against their causes that are dear to their hearts.

When it comes to extremists in this country, the causes may be a little harder to see, but they are there. Legal immigration and other governmental activities that are leading to a growth in diversity are threatening the members of these groups, with their need for supremacy. In a report given to Congress earlier this year, former FBI director Louis Freeh states that right-wing extremists form the basis of the domestic terrorism threat currently facing American citizens.

In some ways, it all comes down to a fear of change, an inability to accept the equality of others that must be the result of feelings of personal inadequacy. People who are not secure about who they are need to attack others who are different than themselves, and who are therefore seen as threats. And this is true not just of those who differ from us in race, nation origin, gender, religion or other categories. It can also be directed against homosexuals.

Hate crimes against gay men and women have made themselves known in horrifying ways. We all know of Eric Rudolph, who is still on the run for his murder at an abortion clinic. He is also implicated in attacks on customers in a gay bar. His religious ideology led him to attack those he sees as living counter to his own statement of faith in how the world should be run. This leads directly to a fourth reason for extremism and terrorism in the United States:

*Religion and ideology.* One of the right-wing factions named as a domestic terrorism threat is the Christian Identity movement because it condones religiously motivated racism and violence. Former FBI chief Louis Freeh says that "identity beliefs are increasingly found in the rhetoric of all types of right-wing extremist groups, including, but not limited to . . . survivalist communes, the Ku Klux Klan, neo-Nazis, skinheads, tax protesters and common law courts. All believe that government no longer protects their own self-interest to be the ones who rule and prosper.

The latest attacks against abortion clinics are the perfect example of how ideology can lead to terrorism. Some anti-abortion advocates have resorted to violent acts, such as vandalism, bombings, and murder. A recent survey released by the feminist Majority Foundation found that, in the first part of 1998 alone, 22% of abortion clinics experienced some form of violence or threat of violence.

The danger at abortion clinics has escalated to such a degree that the White House is proposing protection. Abortion clinics are asking for funds for bulletproof windows, closed-circuit camera systems, and alarm systems. Washington is seeking $4.5 million to help clinics install such security measures and to pay for studies that can determine which clinics are most at risk. We all know that the topic of abortion is extremely controversial, but most of us can agree that more violence is not the answer. The creation of violence in order to prevent violence is not rational. It is a sad fact that violence at abortion clinics is almost expected these days and does not come as much of a surprise to anybody.

In fact, recent religious movements within domestic terrorism movements have gone to new ground, with racist versions of multi-ethnic paganism like Odinism on the rise. Foreign terrorism often has a religious basis, as adherents fight "holy wars" that take no prisoners, and ask no quarter.

*Globalism.* Because of technology, the world is changing quickly, moving from local to global, from static to changeable, from agricultural to electronic, from like-me to diverse. It's overwhelming, and terrorists want to hold on to what they know, and what worked well for them in ages past. All sides sometimes coalesce to fight globalism, or transnational capitalism. This battle can hook into the rage of persons of diverse economic doctrines.

Because they do not have the idea of economic gain and are willing to sacrifice all for the cause, along with their extreme loyalty to each other, terrorists and extremists are very dangerous.

## WHAT CAN WE DO ABOUT IT?

Is there any way of identifying the type of person who is capable of such terrorism? Probably not. However, there has been in the past a consistent profile of America's domestic terrorists. They are generally part of extremist groups, which are found in almost every city in the United States. Although their target may not be the World Trade Center, the choice of a group from the Middle East, they could mark any local church or business as a tempting target.

Extremists share this basic attitude: anything for the cause. They are willing to sacrifice anything—their freedom, their security, and even their lives and those of others—in pursuit of their goal.

They also usually field a more public side that helps in attracting new converts, but they are also run by a secretive core group that is difficult to penetrate.

One thing that will help is a coordinated effort. While terrorist groups are advancing in their technological aims, local law enforcement officers geared to fight against them are suffering from a lack of a database of intelligence and a lack of "connectivity." That's why we need a coordinated effort: Terrorists and extremists usually work in small, efficient, and covert groups that are secure, mobile and travel extensively. They usually have support groups that will protect and sustain them in many areas, as well as provide fake documents.

Different police and enforcement venues may have different pieces of the puzzle that must be coordinated and brought together before a true picture of the terrorist activity can be discerned. That is why prevention and enforcement efforts must all strive for this "connectivity." We must guard against duplicating efforts, wasting resources and focus more on "combined intelligence" of information.

We must continue to be aware of the terrorist groups in our area so that we can uncover terrorist plots that are close to home. Recently, in California, for example, authorities discovered two Pacific Gas & Electric Company warehouses filled with bomb making materials described as "ready-to-go explosives," complete with instruction manuals.

The first bomb-making operation site was discovered when a PG&E employee found a trail of water in a warehouse basement. He found that it led to 250 pounds of ammonium nitrate thawing inside a locker. Fearing the worst, police ordered the 30 workers out of the building and also evacuated one nearby. Police initially questioned one worker about the operation. That worker soon led them to a second building with a similar bomb-making setup. The worker, who was not arrested, had no criminal record. It was later found that another worker at the plant was responsible for making the bombs. He was arrested, although he did not appear to have a political agenda.

The man claimed the explosives were intended to be used as fireworks. Coincidentally, his firework formula was the same as that used to create the bombs that caused the terrorist disaster in Oklahoma City. Can you imagine how it must feel to find out from the news that a man you have worked beside every day is responsible for making potentially deadly (whether or not that's his intention) explosives?

But in order to present a united front against anti-governmental terrorism, education is needed. The government, including the FBI, State Department, FAA and others, has put together a wealth of information on statistics that can point to trends, new threats and potential solutions.

In addition, there are many things we can do to help with the aftermath of terrorism. To prevent seemingly helpless situations, in 1983, Jeffrey Mitchell, an expert in crisis intervention, began teaching a group crisis-intervention technique. The goals of this critical incident stress that debriefing program are to "mitigate the impact of a traumatic event" and to accelerate the normal recovery process of healthy people, both victims and rescue workers, who have been exposed to very unusual events." The members of the CISU programs form teams that perform interventions that provide eight different services:

- Getting traumatized people to talk about their experiences (studies support this practice, as they show that talking about a traumatic event can actually serve as a calming mechanism and enhance the immune system's ability to cope)

- One-on-one contact with the individuals, usually within 72 hours of the event
- Instituting organizational and personnel resources, including calling in grief counselors or other members of the mental health field
- Taking over for those who are unable to make crucial decisions
- Helping people to realize that their reactions are normal and that they needn't be ashamed of their feelings
- Restoring social ties—helping people to see that others have shared this experience so that they won't feel alone
- Providing direction with practical stress-management knowledge
- Helping people to regain control by aiding their business in resuming normal function as soon as possible

These services, which were in operation at the Oklahoma City disaster, train people to face a crisis and get back on their feet again, while making them feel as comfortable and safe as possible.

One woman who helped in the rescue efforts in Oklahoma City—there were a thousand injured as well as 168 dead—had a lot to say about what the disaster showed her.

The work was done with speed and with accuracy, she said, and it involved crane operators, construction companies, restaurateurs, veterinarians, doctors, engineers, and so many others. The FBI, ATF, FEMA and the police all acted professionally. The townsfolk worked for rescue units from other cities by feeding them, clothing them and comforting them. People would vomit from the smell, danger, and exhaustion, and keep working without rest. And despite damage to doors that would not lock, there was not one instance of looting.

This kind of reaction in Oklahoma was a good precursor to what would happen at Ground Zero in New York, and at the Pentagon and on Flight 93. Americans working together without rest, without fear and with total compassion. And it happened beyond that, in cities across America.

One special group of victims in this case was the American Muslim community, religiously true to the fundamentals of their religion, which preaches compassion and charity, and to the ideals of the United States for freedom and bravery. There were too many unfortunate events targeting those who follow Islam, beatings and mosque defacing, but at the same time there were ecumenical services, neighbors helping neighbors, and a new understanding of what our Muslim friends truly believe.

Bob Brubaker published a guide for those who must deal with adversity and how we can best recover in the wake of terrorism, and these are good words for us to hear in an America torn apart and working to heal itself:

1. Focus on allowing God to comfort us.
2. Focus on the other people who are trying to help you. Do not push others away in your grief.
3. Focus not on what is gone, but on what is left.
4. Focus on what is important—and use disaster as a wake-up call to reassess what that might be and how you can begin a new life by learning what to make central in it.

Terrorists—all terrorists—try to scare us into giving up control of our lives. Let's do our best to take it back. The only way to protect yourself and others is to be aware, be prepared, and be ready. You never know who will be the terrorist's next victim. Who's to say that it won't be you or someone you know or love?

**Chapter IX**

# CONSUMER RAGE:
# RAGE AGAINST THE MACHINE

Not all terrorists are part of an extremist group raging against the government, as we have seen proven many times over the years. Sometimes, the enemy is the corporate or technological world, be it a multinational giant or Sam's Drug Store down on the corner. When an issue is strongly emotional, it is not difficult for people to lose control and wage an undeclared or even a declared war against business. Take, for instance, riots and other forms of civil disorder.

We've witnessed them, if not at first hand, then on television, too many times. We see that the people who take part in the rioting haven't always planned their actions. They may simply become caught up in their surroundings and become so emotional that they turn violent.

However, more and more, riots are seen as a legitimate form of social protest. They are planned. And many of those who participate want to do far more than to make a statement. Some just want a free TV. Others want to hurt people, no matter whom. Many seek publicity and a voice that is heard over as far a reach as possible. And all want to obstruct business as usual and keep it obstructed for as long as possible.

The riots of early in the last century were often generated by labor unrest, and those of the late last century were generally the result of civil rights protest. But the turn of the century has so far been marked by riots, at home and abroad, that are largely the result of social activists concerned about a number of things, and taking these concerns to the street with an attack on any neighboring business or passerby. Perhaps the biggest riots in recent history were the World Trade Organization riots in Seattle, Quebec, Switzerland and Italy, with a riot in Genoa that left one person dead.

Unfortunately, differences of opinion that should be resolved through discussion and democratic means are instead brought to the forefront of public scrutiny through riots and illegal acts that work to disrupt commercial and social activity at every level. Much of the effort behind these riots and similar acts of violence involves activity against newer technologies. Indeed, the aftermath of the WTO riot in Seattle led to a new formation of neo-Luddites, a group which echoes the Luddite movement in early nineteenth-century England that worked to counter the effects of the Industrial Revolution.

There are biotechnology and nanotechnology terrorists who have targeted genetically modified foods and even grass seeds, doing much damage at a seed research facility in Oregon. There are also the anti-business activities of radical ecologists such as Earth First! and the Earth Liberation Front, which torched a $12 million ski resort in Vail, Colorado. Others have sabotaged equipment or booby trapped trees to kill loggers. Animal research lab break-ins and throwing acid or paint on passersby in fur coats are an old story for animal rights activists. So are meat departments in food stores and greyhound race tracks. The Animal Liberation Front has released thousands of brown trout from an English research center and broke windows and threatened arson against agencies selling tickets to a traveling circus that had animal entertainers. With this kind of broad-based rage, almost any type of business could be targeted.

Of course, activists targeting these causes are, for the most part, working through their organizations to get their message across and change people's minds in peaceful ways. But not all. And that is where activities such as riots, break-ins and sabotage begin.

The anti-technological, anti-business stance can also be seen in the activities of a terrorist such as Ted Kaczynski, the Unabomber, who killed three people and wounded 23 others in 16 attacks. Publication of his 35,000-word manifesto in 1995 led to his capture. This is intellectual rage, wherein the actor is so enamored of his own worldview that he must perform, and by force, impose it on others.

## WHY DO RIOTS HAPPEN?

Riots and other rage against the machine activities take place because of discomfort with the speed of change. To many, the world is going too fast. It is said that the power of technology, such as the capabilities of computers, doubles itself every month. Anyone who has ever tried the old bar trick of betting someone that they can't place kernels of corn on a chessboard and double the amount of corn on each square would understand how quickly the amount of computer power would increase. This kind of change is seen as frightening to some, liberating to others.

The speed of change, called Future Shock, makes many people uncomfortable. They feel that they have lost the ability to control their environments, and this feeling of powerlessness means that they must cast about for an enemy or a scapegoat that would explain this loss. After all, lost power must have gone somewhere and have been regained by someone else.

One interesting thing about the forces against economic globalism is that they combine the interests of both the political far right and the political far left. The effort is a true incidence of extremism, with extremes on both ends of the political spectrum taking part. They regard themselves as truly free peoples fighting for liberty against the oppressor, the police state and free-trade corporate interests. And the corporation is seen as any for-profit business activity, even the landlord, as activists proclaim "rent is theft." Alliances are forming between members of both sides, as they share some surprising commonalities, such as hatred of capitalism and centralization.

All are brought together in the so-called Third Position, neither capitalism nor communism but a third way. That way lies in decentralization of political and economic power and the redistribution of wealth, to smaller, homogenous and autonomous groups. An amalgamation of left and right also champions such issues as ecology, labor movement and animal rights. Both sides also share a renewed interest in paganism, in a falling away from traditionalism that rivals the falling away from traditional economics and politics.

Many on both sides of the spectrum are now finding themselves in agreement. They dislike such capitalistic practices as the charging of interest, with some taking a strong Anti-Semitic stance on this. This is because Christians in the Middle Ages were forbidden to charge interest as the church believed money, being non-organic, could not reproduce, so banking and the levying of interest became the province of the Jews. Anti-Semitism by debtors followed.

There are also many on both sides who argue against multi-culturalism and immigration, whether it leads to mongrelization of races or promotion of similarities. So they are likely to champion groups like the Nation of Islam, and nations with terrorist policies such as Iraq and Libya. Rage against government and business come together in their stance.

It's odd to think of the right-wing as a proponent of environmental activism, but the movement goes back to Hitler's mystical love for the clean mountains of the homeland and the virtues of a rugged outdoor life, shared by many of those, right and left, who hide out in the countryside and live off the land.

And it may be odd to think of the left as being anti-immigration, but in a 1998 media-fiasco, some 40% of the Sierra Club voted to resolve that immigration was an environmental ill. The author of the radical environmental guidebook, *The Monkey Wrench Gang*, cried out against immigration by "culturally-morally-genetically impoverished" people.

These beliefs are all totally legal, but the way some of their proponents choose to act on them is not. Riots and illegal activities are the result of rage. And this kind of rage against the machine has to be brought to public attention in order to enlist as many converts as quickly as possible. Therefore, publicity is essential. While pronouncements may go unheard and manifestos may go unnoticed (unless one is Ted Kaczynski and is holding the world's attention hostage with violent actions), a riot or violent act will quickly gain the attention of the media. What's more, it is far easier and more fun than reasoned logic.

Rioting allows rioters to disturb the ongoing flow of life, giving them control over the situation. It is odd to think of something as chaotic as an element of control, as it is so obviously an uncontrolled environment, but the control stems from the power that the rioters are taking. They are taking over, and exhibiting power against those they feel have had the power up until now, and who have marginalized them. In riots, it seems to the rioters that they are the ones who have the power, when in actuality, no one has the power, and no one can really control the event.

## "I Just Want Basic Good Service"

But you don't have to be a Luddite to have some rage against the machine or want to destroy industrial society to want to throw your computer over a cliff. While riots by the politically motivated neo-Luddite who wants to do away with technology and world trade may gain a lot of attention, rage against the machine is much more prevalent in everyday life. It is a rage felt by a lot of people who are otherwise pretty much happy with the way things are. They love their cell phones, VCRs, DVDs and so on, except not always.

It is the rage felt by customers who cannot get their needs met. This is the rage felt by a Connecticut man who had trouble getting a bank to rescind some inappropriate charges on his phone account, although he called and wrote time and time again. This kind of rage is made of long lines and long waits and that ubiquitous press-three-for-further-options message you get on the phone when you call customer service. He would have loved to get a person on the other end, but he had no such luck.

This rage costs businesses plenty. McDonald's estimates that rude employees cost at least $750 million last year, and that is a 3.8% loss of revenue. Companies as diverse as The Container Store, Tom's of Maine and Southwest Airlines are using tactics that result from ethics based organizational philosophies, such as the Container Store's idea that they are "morally obligated to help customers solve problems and not just sell them products" earned the firm sales increases of 20% to 25%.

I am often asked what separates my business from the rest. First, we have human beings answering the phone, and that can take your customer satisfaction ratings to great heights. Automation is not always the answer.

Secondly, we do one thing very well. That one thing is that we return phone calls and we do it within 24 hours and hopefully sooner. I have a return phone call policy for all my employees. The policy simply is return all phone calls within 24 hours, even the ones they don't want to make or the people who call and they don't like. I tell my employees to call the person they don't like and tell them they don't like them, but they must do it within 24 hours.

Finally, my company will send people we meet, do business with and who refer us additional business thank-you notes every time one of those events take place. Why? Because it is the right thing to do since someone took some time and effort to make your life better and potentially more prosperous.

Do you want to spend $10,000 to $50,000 a year on advertisements telling people how great your company is or do you just need to show them in such very simple ways you care and appreciate all their effort, time and business?

## WE'RE CONDITIONED TO EXPECT TERRIBLE SERVICE

Different surveys have been taken, and they show that today, the average American does not expect good service. However, those businesses that embrace great service or even good service are experiencing a surge in customer loyalty. In fact, price falls from the number one reason for utilizing a service.

I had a unique experience one day. I was dressed sloppily since I was working on my home and I expected to be engaged in dirty repairs all day. With my son in hand, I went to a home repairs supply company with the intent to spend a considerable amount of money. We walked up and down several rows of products and by several store employees, with not one asking if I needed assistance. Finally, I stopped two store employees who were just chatting with each other and I asked them where a certain product was. To my dismay, one of them pointed to a certain direction and told me to turn up the aisle and look about halfway up.

I said "thanks," and my son and I promptly walked pass several aisles and out the door, never to return. This store has since gone out of business, and who could guess why?

My son and I promptly went to another home supply store, Home Depot, where we experienced a totally different experience, so good that I will not shop anywhere else but there, and price is not even a factor at all.

While my son and I were at Home Depot, I bought two large trashcans along with the other products we originally needed to buy. Within 30 days, the trash can handle had broken off. Of course, I had no receipt and was angry that I most likely would have to buy another trashcan. So, I loaded up my broken trashcan and my son. I thought this was a good time to teach my son how to demand a product exchange without a receipt. I had the mentality of a linebacker waiting for the ball carrier.

I arrived at Home Depot, dragging the trashcan behind me with my son at my side, anticipating warfare and with the attitude that I have to win and show my son victory can be accomplished. I walked firmly to the "Return" Counter where a young lady was waiting. I explained with a huff that I just bought this trashcan 30 days ago and the handle broke. Before I could get the words out that I don't have my receipt, she said, "Sir"—I was thinking she was going to ask for my receipt and here we go again with typical poor American service—"go pick out a new trashcan and come back to me." Then, she said she will fill out the paperwork for me while I get a new trashcan. Finally, I came back with my new trashcan and was told there was no need for me to go through the regular line. I want to buy EVERYTHING from Home Depot from now on, I thought.

Starbucks has some of the most expensive coffee around. Did you know that their regular customers frequent their coffee shops on an average of 17 times a month? Why? Because they have expensive coffee? No, is it because they have a good-tasting product? That helps, but more importantly, they have the warm and fuzzy service that is unique and consistent. They make you feel like they love each and everyone of their customers.

Part of the reason for the death of good service in this country is that some customers, the more frequent and high-paying ones, get better service, with the marginal and less frequent buyer relegated to a sharing a service rep with thousands of others. This can even extend to the speed of getting service done and products fixed. American Express, for instance, offers a Centurion Card for $1,000 a year to help those who value service over price get concierge service. The Gartner Group has found that 72% of the larger banks planned to divide customers into segments based on their profitability.

It all goes back to when supermarkets took over from the

corner IGA grocer, with more selection but less help in making that selection. These were followed by the big box stores, where you were pretty much in charge of your own shopping. They offered bargains, but with some loss of the personal touch and expertise of the shopkeeper.

However, technology can also be used positively, to allow the customer to track his own transactions. We do this whenever we call an 800 number, punch in some code numbers and see which checks have cleared our account or transfer funds from savings to checking without leaving the house. Shippers can look on a computer to see just where their shipment is and when it will arrive.

Technology is also being used to make each customer a unique individual, with web sites telling you about some interesting item meant just for you—gleaned from your buying history. Continental Airlines has a system that lets each reservation agent know of your history and value, so you are informed about remedies for problems you may have and perks you are entitled to.

Although some may miss the day when a living person took care of you, those persons were an expensive part of doing business, and the cost of doing that business has been substantially reduced, with a lowered price for consumers. That is why we are seeing banks that require us to have automatic deposits and do not send us back cancelled checks, vendors who request that automatic payments be made from out accounts, and phone companies that give us big discounts for sending us our detailed bill, with interactivity that lets us see who belongs to all those numbers we called online.

For every consumer that complains, there are many who like the price, and who patronize such web sites as priceline.com to offer their own prices for tickets and hotel rooms.

But the Internet is not always a benign presence. It can bring into your home the same dangers that the TV can, but far more clandestinely. It is known that Eric Harris of Columbine fame learned to make his bombs on the Internet, and there is a wealth of information there for other terrorists. Today's instant and totally connected media offers students a primer on how to hold a school hostage, and violent video games give them the quick reflexes they need to use their weapons.

The Internet is also a boon to militias and other terrorist groups who use it to keep in touch, share horror stories of ill treatment, and spread their messages to enlist others. The computer has been called a vital piece of equipment to extremists everywhere. Of course, not the least of the danger is the hacker, be he a solo practitioner or terrorist, who breaks into government, utility or company computers to steal information or to damage the ability of the computer to do business as usual. It is electronic rioting.

That pasty-faced kid with the Pepsi and Fritos can be visiting his rage against society onto you in the form of a virus that can strike with no warning, and replicate itself in the bowels of all machines you come into contact with. Viruses and worms are just another form of rage, meant to destroy and discombobulate for the enjoyment of those who produce them.

Technology and the computer can also be used by the outraged for cyber stalking, the practice of using the Internet to reach out and harass someone. It can take the form of threatening behavior or unwanted advances directed at another via email, live chat harassment, the online verbal abuse known as flaming, spamming, which means sending a barrage of junk email, or leaving improper messages on bulletin boards or in guest books. One very scary scenario involves the ease by which computers can be used to commit identify theft. A relatively new phenomenon, it is being fueled by the decreasing expense of computers and online services.

Technology can be used to steal what is most essential to ourselves—our basic identity. Scott Lewis, a Kent, Ohio resident, had everything going for him . . . until he began to be shunned—and even feared—by potential employers. After trying repeatedly to get the jobs he was highly qualified for, Scott settled for a low-paying job. He also hired me to run a background check on himself, and through that check found that a murder charge and several DUI charges were attached to his social security number.

How did Scott's social security number get linked to a stranger's record? Ten years earlier, a database entry mistake attached Scott's ID to a man arrested for driving under the influence.

Similar to off-line stalking, online stalking can terrify victims, placing them in psychological trauma, and in fear of physical harm. Many cyberstalking situations end up in real-life stalking, with the victim getting abusive and excessive phone calls, vandalism, threatening mail, trespassing and assault. Oh brave new world, which has such people in it.

Because there is so much personal information available online, legislators are beginning to address the problem. Off-line stalking laws are being extended to cover online communication, as are anti-harassment laws. States such as Alabama, Arizona, Connecticut, Hawaii, Illinois, New Hampshire, and New York specifically include the electronic transmission of such communications in their anti-harassment legislation, while California, Oklahoma, Wyoming, and Alaska have placed them in their anti-stalking laws. Federal legislation has been introduced, championed by former vice president Al Gore.

A recent news story shows what else can be done to threaten people. An anti-abortion group posted a list of abortion providers on a site amid incendiary graphics and included home addresses and phone numbers, automobile descriptions, license plate numbers, and other personal details. Providers who had been killed had a line drawn through their name, and those wounded were listed in gray. Though the site did not advocate murder specifically, it was linked to a letter from an abortion-doctor murderer who talked of how good it felt to do the killing.

Suit was brought by Planned Parenthood against the site's sponsor, and a jury agreed: this was a threat, and it awarded Planned Parenthood over $100 million.

# How to Prevent or Reduce These Problems

As we are seeing riots and other illegal political acts more and more often on the nightly news, corporations are becoming one of the hardest hit targets of outraged rioters. It would be wise for any business that is concerned about preventing a violent attack to do some research on any locally known extremist groups, and to keep careful track of any threats and methods used by these groups.

Most riots, even those based on social activism, share a common pattern, as pointed out by Allan M. Apo, CPP, of *Security Management* magazine. For example, during civil disorders, the systems that normally protect us are generally unable to function properly. Police and firefighting departments are so busy that it is unlikely that any one business will be able to obtain their immediate help.

According to Ronald Mendell, author of an article in *Security Management* magazine, intelligence gatherers can exploit several different aspects of terrorist groups, such as their problems with displeased members, insecure information systems, and their need to produce propaganda. Once this information is known, it can be used in conjunction with law enforcement and private security systems to protect a business from possible attacks. Information of this kind can also determine when and where an extremist group may strike, and so you can then formulate the best possible ways to protect company personnel and property.

Security professionals should also keep track of local extremist groups by reading their propaganda, attending their rallies, identifying their leaders, and working with other security professionals. It is much better to have a preventative plan in place to protect employees from extremist attacks than to merely have an emergency plan to be used when it is too late.

However, most businesses have not thought about how they would respond to a terrorist disaster. John Lobe, a crisis management and workplace violence consultant who was on hand at the time of the Oklahoma City bombing, stresses that the effectiveness of a business' response depends on whether or not it already has an active plan for people to follow. He says: "Businesses that choose to deny that incidents will—or might—happen minimize the importance of having a plan. They put the cost of setting up the program over the value of helping their personnel." Without having a plan ready, the only way a company can respond is during a very unnatural situation, and the only result will be utter chaos.

So, what is the key to being successful in a disastrous situation? It's simple. Education. Training. Crisis intervention author Max Siporin defines a disaster as "an extreme social crisis situation in which individuals and their social systems become dysfunctional and disorganized, sustain personal, collective and public hardships, and also become a 'community of sufferers.'"

In a riot or other emergency action, not only are outside resources spread so thin that they don't work, inside resources, such as corporate managers and trained emergency personnel are also drained. Something they must learn is that the stress of a crisis can (and will) affect a person's performance. Without this understanding, they tend to underestimate how critical their roles are in the company's survival of a dangerous situation.

So how can you protect yourself in a situation where no outside help is available? By being knowledgeable about past rioting trends and learning from them. Places that are looted are attacked under some form of order. Retail businesses are the looter's and the arsonist's first target. The most likely places to be looted first are pawnshops and liquor stores. (Just what we need . . . drunken looters and arsonists.) Food markets (again, mostly for their supply of liquor and cigarettes) are the next likely to be attacked, followed by drug stores, clothing stores, appliance stores, and furniture stores. Looters always give top priority to anything that can be easily moved. And they normally stick to inner-city businesses where they can be defended and protected by their neighborhoods and friends.

The following advice has also proven to be a consistent factor in dealing with riot situations:

- Looting and arson prevention will reduce loss, as some damaged goods may still be recoverable.
- Occupied businesses are less likely to fall under attack.
- Preventative public relations may be the biggest asset in controlling its environment.

Jeffrey Mitchell, an expert in crisis intervention, teaches a group crisis intervention technique meant to mitigate the impact of a traumatic event. It is being used in commercial, industrial, military, and educational settings as participants are trained by a cooperative group of crisis counselors, psychologists, corporate leaders, and business consultants. Originally created for emergency response personnel, a growing number of businesses are getting involved so they can be prepared if a catastrophe emerges in their companies.

Managers are told that they can help by reuniting survivors, encouraging them to accept tasks regarding their own care, encouraging people to talk about their ordeal, providing basic shelter and necessities, especially privacy, providing food and rest to rescuers, providing accurate and up-to-date information when possible, being honest, being with victims to support them, assigning a media spokesperson to deal with the press, and calling in a crisis intervention team.

Exposing a team of members at a company to such training, it is said, will help ensure a much safer and smoother transition for everyone in the case of a terrorist attack.

But there are other measures that businesses should take to prepare themselves in case of emergency. Here is a checklist:

- If you have security forces and equipment such as fences to help protect you, check them on a regular basis to ensure their stability.
- Companies can use deterrent strategies such as making

sure that their building is well illuminated. A building that looks well lit implies that it is occupied, and is much less likely to fall under attack than a poorly lit, unoccupied building.

- Give special consideration to fire prevention measures. Vandalism and firefighting operations can affect the water supply, rendering sprinkler systems useless. And sprinkler systems with outside control valves can often be shut off by rioters! If a riot is expected, locking sprinkler control systems or removing the hand wheel from the control valve when it is in the open position are steps that can help ensure the accessibility of water.

- Roofs should also be equipped with fire extinguishers suitable for flammable liquid fires, and employees should be trained in their proper use.

- All other fire fighting equipment, such as mobile fire carts and sand pails, should also be checked regularly.

- Keep duplicates of their vital bookkeeping and insurance information off the premises and at a secure location. Losing such records in a riot or other emergency situation alone is enough to potentially shut a company down. In addition to keeping track of past financial and business records, these duplicates are incredibly valuable in establishing true losses and business interruption claims. They can also help to identify stolen goods by means of markings, such as serial numbers. If no numbers are available to keep track of, a company may want to use Operation Identification, which involves imprinting all valuable property with a recognizable number, such as a social security number.

- If a riot is suddenly expected and a business is left with little time to vacate, target inventories such as cash, jewelry, high-priced items, liquor and drugs, and guns should be immediately removed or placed in a secure place, out of sight.

- If an office safe is used to secure valuable items, it should be just that—secure. It should be something that cannot be easily moved.

- If a business is given adequate warning that rioting may occur, it should try to reduce its entire inventory. If time permits, merchandise should also be removed from displays that are visible from the street, and the windows themselves should be protected.
- Precut plywood boards and steel rolling shutters are the best means of protection against attack.
- All entrances and exits should also be sealed off from public access, while still leaving escape routes for employees who may not be able to make it out of the building and for emergency personnel access. Don't forget to seal other openings, such as skylights, trash chutes, and ventilator openings.
- Elevator cars should also be sent to the upper floors and should be made inoperable, if allowed by the fire department.
- If there is enough time, other precautions should also be made, such as removing flammable liquids from the area, shutting off the gas supply, and moving company vehicles.
- Evacuation routes for employees should be determined beforehand, and all employees should be properly notified of them.
- They should also be instructed on evacuation safety measures. They should be reminded that, when driving out of the area, all car windows should be rolled up and the doors locked. And drivers need to be aware of alternate routes they can take, in case their regular routes are in the path of violence.
- If it is unsafe to evacuate, all buildings should have a "safe room" where employees and customers can hide to wait out the danger. These rooms should be equipped with a phone, preferably a cellular phone (in case phone lines are down), so that they can communicate with the

authorities and notify them of their location. And to ensure that the lines of communication stay open, names and phone numbers of emergency departments, security officers, transit authorities, and company officials should be posted throughout the building.

• Battery-operated radios should also be available, in case all other forms of communication are down.

However, it is said that maybe the most important way a company can protect its assets is to form good relationships within its community. Good public relations will establish mutual trust. In fact, if this is the case, a member of the community might even tip off a business if it is in danger of becoming the victim of a riot.

These precautions may seem unnecessary, but they are a small price to pay considering the lives that they may save. It is much better for everyone's interest that companies make these preparations in advance. If they don't, they may find themselves unable to operate safely in the event of an emergency. Even a person with the best intentions can be stripped of rational thinking by a traumatic event.

Overall, government and industry, because they are targeted by the same forces of opposition, need to work more closely together to solve the problem of rioting. They need to operate in the same world, rather than in two different ones. Ambassador Anthony Quainton says that "much of the violence is against the public sector; therefore, a partnership has to be a two-way street in information sharing as well as technology sharing." In addition, Quainton describes a new government bureau that will be developed to collectively address terrorism, crime, and narcotics, and to study how these issues affect both private and public security.

Victims of cyber-stalking should send the stalker, if known, a clear written warning, just as those in the physical world do, that the contact is unwelcome and that he should stop it. Then, no matter what, the victim should ignore all communication from the stalker but should save any further communication in electronic and hard copy, recording dates and times. Never, ever meet with the stalker to work things out. Victims can file a report with the local law enforcement or see if the local prosecutor can pursue charges. Victims should also lodge a complaint with their own and the stalker's service provider.

If harassment continues, consider changing the email address, service provider, home phone number and look into encryption software or privacy protection programs. A local software store may be able to help. Victims should also remove their names from directories, such as *www.switchboard*.com. Also, they should remember to ask for support from friends, family and victim service professionals.

## A Bend in the Road: One Victim's Story of Survival, Healing and Triumph

What a beautiful September morning it was—warm sunshine, fresh tropical fruits for breakfast, steel drums playing Caribbean melodies. My mother and I had gained a sense of peace, tranquility and rejuvenation during our four-day excursion to the Florida Keys. Little did I know that this morning would mark the end of my life as I knew it.

It was a hard summer—a heart-wrenching breakup and difficulties in my graduate studies. I was about to take a vacation and a much-needed break from my job as a news producer. I just wrapped up a story about tourist safety in the United States that would be aired on television in Europe. A recent rash of tourist-directed crimes in Florida had the attention of all the news media—both within and outside the country—so I produced a news segment providing European vacationers useful tips to ensure their safety. By the time I reached the airport, I was certain that I had everything I needed for the trip: a suitcase of summer clothes, good books to read, some music to play in the rental car and a heightened awareness of how to be safe while in Florida.

The vacation was all that I imagined it could be. My mother and I connected, laughed and spent our days talking and enjoying life together. Mom and I were always close, but her comfort, support and friendship meant everything to me at one of the most difficult times of my life. And when it was time to leave, we got into our rental car and put some big band music on— free-spirited, happy tunes to mark the end of our adventure together—and headed up the highway to Miami International Airport.

We approached the airport with plenty of time before our flights would depart, so we took our time to find the car rental return. At eleven in the morning, we didn't think much of the potential risk in driving around the airport area, but still we were cautious. The streets were busy, and people were striding down the sidewalks. Everything appeared normal, but there was a problem. We couldn't find the lot for our return. It wasn't long before we knew we were heading too far off the beaten path, so I pulled over to turn around, only to find a car pulled up right next to ours, blocking my turn completely.

Within seconds, both of the men in the car had jumped out, smashed through my window, pulled the horn out of the steering column and started to beat my head and neck. My mother was paralyzed with fear, unable to help in any way, as I received blow after blow.

What they were after wasn't clear. When we offered to give them the car and our belongings, the only response was, "Shut up, bitch, we are going to kill you." What was clear was that if we didn't find a way out, we would be murdered by enraged thugs.

In Germany, there is an expression of being "lucky in your unlucky circumstance," and during the assault, I would feel the meaning of that saying. It was when I received a muscle-ripping bite to my left arm that I would have my lucky break in the assailant's attention so that I could free myself from his grip, punch in defense and put the car into drive. They hung on for a while, to the car, and then to me, but eventually they let go and we raced through red lights until we reached the airport terminal and a "place of safety."

When it was all over, I was left with a dislocated jaw, a bloody bite wound and neck injuries so severe that doctors estimated another three millimeters of damage would have rendered me quadriplegic. The wounds from this violent attempt to end my life changed my life and understanding of pain. From that day on, I would live every day with some degree of pain and discomfort, migraine headaches that would incapacitate me at times, a scar of teeth marks that would serve as a constant reminder of the nightmare and a relationship with my mother that would be strained and would never be the same.

My time in the hospital was followed by years of physical therapy and continues on today as I manage the injury and pain that is an integral part of who I am now. The doctors explained that, like a rope when it's twisted, there is tension at the other end, and my neck and upper back injury lead to lower back and hip pain and bursitis as well. I walked with a limp for nearly two years. Every morning for the first year of my recovery, the first conscious moment I experienced was marked by excruciating pain. My dislocated jaw and shattered disk prohibited me from chewing solid foods because doing so would cause my jaw to slide out of place again or lock up altogether. Therefore, I was limited to an essentially liquid and soft food diet. Nerve damage to my left arm and my face meant that parts were numb and would remain without sensation for the rest of my life, and there was a part of me that wished this numbness would spread throughout my entire body—anything to escape the pain.

It was overwhelming. It was depressing. And for the first time in my life, I wanted an escape—any escape from the pain and the nightmare. I drank a lot of alcohol. I let the doctors play with prescription pain medications and muscle relaxants that made my mind so numb that even formulating sentences was difficult. Facing the physical and emotional pain was almost more than I could bear. I contemplated suicide.

Life after returning home was very different. As I started to regain my strength, I began to meet up with my friends and colleagues to try to regain the life I had lived before. As a 24-year old woman, I was pretty sure that getting "back to life" would be the best medicine for me. I needed to go dancing at clubs in the city, have dinner and catch up with friends I had not seen for a while, go to fall classes and try to forget what had happened. But that would be impossible. Dancing was too painful and sitting in class for hours triggered severe spasms in my back. As I talked with friends and family, the question "What did they [the assailants] want?" would often come up, followed by an incredulous "That's crazy" when I explained that the perpetrators responded to us only with death threats. I knew I wasn't crazy and what happened wasn't either, but for most of us, it was hard to make sense of the senseless. But the questions were difficult and made me realize how separated I was from "normal" people or at least those who had never gone through such an intense trauma. They could look at this and try to make some logical conclusions. I only knew the facts of what happened and that there was nothing we could have done to prevent what happened or to lessen the brutality of the assailants.

As weeks passed and my healing was under way, I found that the process of building a new life and understanding of the world would be the hardest thing I ever had to do. Friends that I expected to be with me through thick and thin were feeling frustrated with the length of time it was taking me to heal and the depression that had stolen the smile from my face. And then there were others, people I hardly new, that provided unexpected connections and support. Any sense of predictability or stability seemed elusive.

On the law enforcement side of things, I decided early on that I was going to do whatever I could to see justice in this case. At least my being active would help to establish some small sense of having a voice in what was happening. I wanted to work with law enforcement to rid the public of two violent predators. I phoned detectives weekly, I inquired about the investigation, I returned to Florida to revisit the scene of the crime and to identify one of the two assailants from photo lineups, I cried when evidence was "misplaced" and I would often lay awake at night wondering if there would ever be an end to this nightmare.

Unlike me, my mother chose to retreat within. Her means of coping with the trauma was to resist talking about what happened and to try to forget. She refused to talk with investigators or work with prosecutors. She refused to talk with therapists or victim advocates. Although circumstance put the two of us in this nightmare crisis, my mother could not forgive herself for not acting while I was brutally beaten. Her motherly instinct to protect her child was paralyzed and she couldn't bring herself to forgive or forget. The guilt and damage would create a barrier in our relationship that still exists.

The process of working with investigators and the prosecutor's office was anything but predictable. Within weeks of the assault, I was able to identify one of the two assailants. The face that bit through my arm muscle was one I couldn't forget and would not mistake, and so it was that I found my assailant. After identifying the perpetrator, I learned that he was incarcerated for an almost identical crime during which he bit another victim, this time the mother of a police officer, and was caught in the process. Because he was arrested at the scene of that crime, he would be tried, convicted and ordered to serve a sentence for this offense long before I would face him in court.

The investigation was unlike anything I had seen on television, and if there was some guide for what to expect, I never found it. Delay after delay, I waited for this case to go to trial. There were a number of hurdles along the 3-year road to the courtroom. In addition to the lost evidence, there was a 1-year battle to have the defendant tested for HIV that I could have contracted through the bite and additional delays from the prosecutor's office for which I never received an explanation.

Then there were the ultraviolet photographs taken of my bite wound, misplaced for over a year. These special pictures captured the depth and angle of the teeth that cut through my arm, which would be especially important since we now had a suspect and a means to confirm his part in the crime. Since the photos were gone, there would be no testing or confirmation—only more continuances and delays. And then there was a baseball cap I knocked off of the defendant's head that I was sure would provide DNA from perspiration or hair, but that item would never surface in the courtroom because it was lost in the warehouse of evidence, never to be found. The years of waiting for this investigation to lead to a trial were frustrating for me, but I was also concerned that the lag in time would violate the defendant's right to a speedy trial and could mean he might not be held accountable for what he did. Thankfully, since he was serving time for another crime and conviction, time was not on his side.

The trial finally came after lineups, interviews, depositions, flashbacks, nightmares, tears and physical struggles to learn to live with and carry my body with minimal pain. I made my way back to Miami alone. My family was in denial about what had happened and urged me to "let it go," and "get over it," and discouraged me from working with the criminal justice system they were convinced would fail our family and me. With no personal support, I entered the courtroom alone and I was in total terror. Detectives and prosecutors tried to reassure me that everything would be just fine, but as I waited outside of the courtroom, with the defendant's mother and sister staring at me from across the corridor, I was certain I would die. They would kill me, he would kill me or I would collapse from the overwhelming fear of facing the would-be murderer again. I didn't pass out and I did testify. I did spend 30 minutes explaining why in one interview I described the defendant as "dark black" and in another as "black." The defense counsel would focus on this so-called variation in my eyewitness account to argue my positive identification and introduce a racial element in the case that was wholly irrelevant.

While I testified, the defendant just sat there staring at me with a little smirk. I tried to stay focused on the jury, as the prosecutor instructed. I tried to stay focused on the facts, because I knew the facts would lead to justice. But all I could feel, see or think of was the defendant sneering at me. I'm sure he thought that by targeting a vacationer, he would have every chance for an acquittal, since most victims that are violently attacked when on vacation choose not to return to pursue justice. But as I sat there in front of him, this was the defining moment of truth, and he was using the only weapon he could bring into the courtroom—that smirk.

As a victim witness, or a victim that was testifying in the case, I was not permitted to observe any other testimony or to remain in the courtroom beyond my account. The defendant, however, was granted the right to observe everything. So, after a few days of testimony, long after I had returned to my home, the jury deliberated for 45 minutes and returned with a guilty verdict to four felony charges. Sentencing took place a few months later and, again, I had to fight for my participation in the criminal justice process by reading an impact statement. I wanted the judge to be clear on how this event had affected my health, life and well being. I was granted the chance to share my statement and was relieved to see the "three-strike" career criminal punished with life in prison.

As years went on, I slowly healed. I was feeling better and doing better emotionally. Therapy helped, both physically and emotionally, and I was able to overcome a lot of the pain and anxiety, but the trauma remained real and ever-present in my life. I would drive around with mace under my leg, "just in case." I didn't want to drive in unfamiliar areas, especially not by myself. I couldn't give people the benefit of the doubt and I struggled to trust and believe in anyone. I doubted my faith in God, wondering how He could have let this happen to my mother and to me—and found my way back to a positive perspective of wondering what God wanted me to learn from this experience. Healing is an evolution and takes a long time.

My relationship with my mother also got better over time. We went on other vacations together, choosing destinations with remarkably low instances of crime. We never really spoke about what happened in any comprehensive way or addressed what the incident had done to our relationship. I understood that my mother had to cope in her own way, but I was also very disappointed that the one person who could have understood what I was going through, the one person who saw terror as I did, the only other person I knew to have her life threatened could not connect with me. The damage this assault had on my relationship with my mother was one of the worst offenses imaginable.

I was a changed person with a new career, new focus and new life objectives years later, when one morning I received an automated call from the Florida Department of Corrections. After eight years, the defendant was returning to Miami for a hearing. It took a few weeks to learn the details of what I came to know as the "3-day loophole" through which my assailant was trying to have his sentence vacated. It seems that the defendant should not have been sentenced as a "three strikes" offender after his conviction in my case. Although there were clearly three felony convictions, or "three strikes," mine was the second sequentially, although it was the third conviction. Only three days marked the time between the attack on my mother and me and his next victim, which ended up being the third felony and second conviction. This accounting does not include the pages-long rap sheet and escalating violent patterns of his previous crimes, both as a juvenile and as an adult. Nonetheless, this technicality meant the penalty would be revisited and I would be forced to return to Florida for the next round in my fight for justice.

Now, with the distance I hoped time would bring between my soul and this nightmare, I was facing the monster again— and this time there was a chance he would go free following the hearing. There was a new prosecutor and a new judge, but the same task of advocating for justice remained. Under the sentencing guidelines, I began a massive hyper-vigilant campaign to find Florida appellate court cases that outlined grounds for going above and beyond sentencing guidelines because of the unusual brutality of the case. I found three, all of which I presented to the judge and all of which the judge accepted. I also launched a media campaign with the help of *America's Most Wanted* and *The John Walsh Show* host John Walsh, who wrote a letter to the Florida State Attorney and the judge, which I then used in a letter-writing campaign to state and federal legislators and the media. I launched guerrilla tactics to apply "gentle pressure" to keep this violent felon off the streets, and it worked. The inmate would return to his prison cell for life—and this time, life meant life, with no chance of parole. At least until that next dreaded phone call, whenever that may happen . . .

## UNDERSTANDING JUSTICE

I've come to understand that working with the criminal justice system is a never-ending—it was my own life sentence, of sorts. Not that I would change my role because I need and want to be an active participant in what happens. But our system is set up to provide defendants—not victims—with every right and opportunity. While my assailant had no concerns about medical coverage, paying rent or even college tuition (with taxpayer money) while in the custody of the state, I was facing $50,000 in medical debt and was struggling to survive physically, emotionally and economically. The imbalance, as seen in the chart below, is obvious and appalling. And yet our legislators and government workers tout lower crime rates (which have more to do with fewer people *reporting* crime than with the actual number of violent acts that take place) and use that as a basis for concluding that we have good services and adequate victim legislation. Clearly there is a need for change and better representation for survivors of violence.

| The Victim | The Defendant |
|---|---|
| Becomes an unwilling participant. | Is presumed to have chosen to engage in unlawful and unjust activity. |
| Is traumatized from the violent act. | Is innocent until proven guilty. |
| Is supported by federal and state | Is supported by the Constitution. |
| Has the right to remain silent. | Has the right to remain silent. |
| Is provided access to local victim assistance bureau, when available. | Has the right to an attorney. |
| Must wait until the state and defense are ready for trial. | Has the right to a speedy trial. |
| Must trust the state to pursue a fair trial. | Has the personal right to a fair trial. |
| Is not always informed of the offender's bail release (two-thirds of all victims are not notified). | Has the right to seek bail release. |
| May not be present while other witnesses testify. | Has the right to ask each witness questions. |
| Must rely on the state to present witnesses. That will make the best case against the defendant. | Has the right to present witnesses to testify on his/her behalf. |
| Has no choice in whether to testify or not. | Can decide whether to testify. |
| Has to trust the state to determine the best course for pursuing justice—and an appropriate sentence for the crime. | Has the right to a jury trial. |
| Has no voice in jury selection. | Can be involved in jury selection. |
| May or may not be informed of a plea agreement and related negotiations. | Has the right to negotiate for and accept a plea agreement. |
| Must assertively pursue the opportunity to read an impact statement at sentencing. | Has the right to appeal a guilty verdict and can file multiple motions for appeal hearings. |
| Can receive support by persons in court, protective orders, restitution, victim advocates, victim compensation, and AIDS testing for defendants. | While incarcerated, can receive free room and board, medical care, a college education or technical training, psychological counseling, access to gym facilities, and access to legal resources. |
| Has no "victim protection program" to relocate or change identity to insure safety. | Can sometimes benefit from the Witness Protection Program where sentences are forgiven and relocation and identity changes are paid for by the state in exchange for witness testimony. |
| Receives no financial support or reparation from tax dollars. | Is supported, incarcerated and rehabilitated with tax dollars. |

Source: U.S. Department of Justice and other public information resources

The issue of reporting crimes is critical. The U.S. Department of Justice reports that teens are victim to violent crime more than any other age group and that 52% of victims of violence in this country don't report their crimes. That means the majority of crime victims don't report the violations against them, making justice through the system impossible for most. Why do so few victims report? Is it that most of these non-reporters are teenagers trapped in homes where domestic violence is commonplace and if reporting were to take place it could risk life or living in their homes? Could it have something to do with prosecutors' wanting to try cases that they can win—so that they will have success in their careers and will be promoted to more prestigious positions—with domestic violence cases being among the hardest to prosecute? Maybe, it has something to do with news headlines that draw attention to acquittals based on technicalities, prosecutors who plea horrible offenses because the trials take too long and cost too much or detectives who have missed some important step in process that forces prosecutors to drop charges?

There are, I believe, two primary barriers to making crime reporting a more regular occurrence.

Domestic violence victims, children and adults, face extremely difficult obstacles. Their "place of safety"—the home—is also where they are repeatedly attacked. Domestic violence cases are difficult, at best, to resolve within our criminal justice system. At worst, victims report only to find the system unsupportive or unresponsive to their cries for help and have to return to an environment hotter than ever. Is it any wonder then, that we have so many teen runaways when teens make up a large percentage of crime victim statistics? Protecting victims of domestic violence needs to be a priority if more reporting is to take place, but little is done from within the system to make this happen.

We also see, time and time again, the system failing the innocent by setting perpetrators free after short insulting sentences, trials that somehow fail to reveal the truth in a way where jurors can make sound decisions, jurors who don't take their responsibility seriously and enormous disparities in punishment for identical offenses. The lack of consistency in sentencing and holding criminals accountable for offenses has compromised the belief by the general public that our system can and will provide a sense of justice.

A good friend of mine whom I'll call Stacy, was in her neighborhood departing from a community meeting when she and a neighbor were faced with two armed assailants. The gun was pointed at her head and after knocking her around and stealing her purse, the assailant escaped. Stacy was horrified. After talking with police, she returned to her home frightened and lost—she had no idea how to begin to protect and make her home safe. Since the attacker had her purse, and since her address was on any number of the contents, Stacy feared her attacker will come to her home to "silence" her or perhaps "finish" what he could not do in the exposed streets.

Stacy's strength and alert attention kept her safe over the coming weeks, but she took on a vigilante attitude of wanting to track down her assailant. Convinced that she had seen him before, she probed the streets, setting up her own system of surveillance. Finally she found him, called the police from her cell phone and saw her perpetrator arrested. She found her attacker and was ready to testify.

It's not very often that the state has such a passionate, detail-oriented witness, but Stacy was ready to see this nightmare through to justice. And when the day came for her to testify, she told her compelling account to the courtroom—as two of the jurors slept! Neither the judge nor the attorneys intervened to remedy the problem, and, despite her eyewitness testimony and all the detective work Stacy had done on her own, the jury failed by ultimately acquitting the assailant who committed the crime.

It's precisely this kind of story that has victims fearful of working with the system. The challenge is to help victims navigate and understand the system well enough so that they will report and work toward the goal of justice. If that doesn't happen, we have no means of accountability and reform by the neighborhood terrors that create so much harm and damage.

With every American having a one-in-five chance of falling victim to violent crime and every woman having a one-in-three chance of being sexually assaulted, there are literally millions at risk. Chances are that you or someone close to you has been violated, beaten, humiliated and treated inhumanely. The violence and hatred expressed in these crimes is not uncommon. And as we study patterns and look for societal ways of dealing with violence, it is in domestic violence situations where we see new generations of enraged violent people bred. Granted, there are many survivors of domestic violence who have gone on to establish peaceful, productive lives. But when we look at the population of incarcerated criminals, we see prisons filled with victims of domestic violence. If there is any hope for rehabilitation for violent offenders, then clearly we need to incorporate programs and treatments to cope with the healing these victims need to experience before they can be productive members of society again.

While we have come a long way with victim rights and while those within our justice system work hard to fight crime and criminals, the societal problems that feed into violence make it almost impossible to keep up with the need for better legislation, stronger laws and better rehabilitation and reintegration programs for the convicted. And with resources stretched and with community pressures for stronger action against crime, mistakes will be made and misdirected energy will be spent creating more frustration and further injustice.

Our system clearly doesn't just fail victims; it isn't a failsafe for defendants either. We see headline news reports of DNA tests revealing that a death row inmate put to death years ago did not commit the heinous crime. There are mothers in jail for 20 or 30 years for drug possession charges, while murderers get three to five years. We have innocent people in prisons and guilty living free in our neighborhoods. There's confusion, a feeling of insecurity and questionable confidence in what our system provides.

As I worked with states attorneys to put one of my two assailants in prison, there were so many aspects of the process that didn't make sense to me. There was and is little support for victims—making the healing process even more challenging. Even now, almost 10 years after I was nearly beaten to death, I continue to hear from prosecutors in Florida that there's another appeal on the table. Working with our justice system is a long and tiring process, but I know there is at least one violent and hateful predator off the streets as a result of my participation and testimony.

## WHAT NEXT?

Like many survivors of trauma, I eventually found my way to the final phase of recovery, which meant that I needed to find a constructive outlet for my energy for what had happened to me. Many choose to volunteer, write in a journal, and donate to support organizations or engage in something else that helps to make some sense of what has happened. Finding a healthy outlet for the experience is what enables us to grow and stretch toward a deeper understanding of the world and us. And, while I wished I could forget and go back in time, the most productive step I could take was to be active in my own recovery and in seeking out justice.

Over the years, it became clear to me that what one community offers in support and services to victims may vary completely from another. In some cases, victims are given monetary reimbursement, psychological counseling, support groups and a victim advocate. In others, victims are left more or less on their own to cope, manage and start the healing process. It was from this gap of disparity that I decided to create the first national nonprofit organization, Witness Justice, providing direct services to all victims of violent crime.

Witness Justice was established in April 2002 and its mission is to empower victims of violent crime with the information, support and tools needed to establish a sense of personal justice and healing. Witness Justice is an organization that serves victims of violent crime by providing information that establishes an understanding of the healing process, justice system and victim rights. It works to empower victims with support and information so that healing can take place. Witness Justice also serves as a portal through which victims can locate local and state supported services, connect with one another for support and ask expert volunteers important questions about recovery and justice.

The Web site (*www.witnessjustice.org*) offers information about every aspect of recovery and healing and provides a means for victims to anonymously connect with others to share experiences, ideas, advice and concerns, and thereby create a sense of understanding, support and community. The virtual community makes it possible for victims to remain anonymous and to explore information and resources in their own time and at a pace that they would feel comfortable with.

By providing a means through which victims can connect with and support one another, it is my hope that survivors can heal and find a new place of happiness. It is also a goal of Witness Justice that more survivors of violent crime will understand the justice system more fully and will therefore come forward with reporting crimes. With a deeper understanding of what is happening, important information about how to begin the healing process and tools for how to navigate the criminal justice system, hopefully more victims will be empowered to pursue their own personal sense of justice and healing.

For more information about Witness Justice or victim support services, please visit the Web site at *www.witnessjustice.org* or call 800-4WJ-HELP.

**Chapter X**

# LIFE RAGE:
# THE ULTIMATE SOLUTION

The chapters that preceded this one have provided not only a definition of the problem of rage and its causes but also some of the solutions people have found to counteract rage. And these solutions appear to be working.

For instance, despite concerns about school violence, a government report shows that it has been dropping since 1993. And not only is crime dropping, with fewer kids committing it and fewer kids victimized by it, numbers like teen childbirth and smoking are down as well, while the numbers of kids vaccinated and in preschool are up. "The trend is in the right direction," said Kristin Moore, president of the research group Child Trends, which has a web site with the good news at *http:/ /childstats.gov*.

Indeed, many experts say that work, road and air rage reflect our need to lump similar events together to create patterns. Others would say that they are self-fulfilling prophecies fueled by the media. Anecdotes are used by the media and others to represent trends that may or may not be borne out by actual statistics. Gallup polls show no increase in the numbers of people who report feeling angry at work, and these were not high to begin with, say pollsters. Air and road rage reflect mainly the increasing numbers of people who travel. Federal aviation authorities have only recorded about 200 incidents in which passengers interfered with flight crews, about one for every three million passengers, not bad odds. What reports of rage actually do is to encourage others to report such activities and events because they now have a name.

This could indeed be good news, if we can only do two things. One is to avoid a sense of overwhelming fear when we hear of such reports. We must remember this: that news is news, and it focuses on the unusual and the outrageous, not on everyday life. The old saw goes that you will not see a headline that says "Dog bites man," but that "Man bites dog" will appear every time it happened. The electronic media has a saying that goes: "If it bleeds, it leads," and so their emphasis will always be on telling us of violent events to attract our interest. You would not stay up to watch News at 11 if it featured the Jones family sitting down to dinner, yet that is a pretty typical event in the ordinary life.

Instead, the media focuses on criminals, terrorists, teens whose lives have gone wrong and even some of the cultural purveyors of negativity in a way that seems to champion and glorify them. But at least, these reports, no matter how negatively presented, are based on actual news. The media also gives us a false impression of what is important in life by focusing on the worst of culture, entertainment reports such as whether some drug addict will be appearing on tonight's leading sitcom that night or tabloid-style articles such as what star is undergoing a life crisis.

The other thing that we need to do is to use these news reports about the various Life Rage categories to make the world a better place. Even if there is no massive epidemic of rage, we can still use this news to help us realize that problems of anger and frustration do exist and do cause problems in the world.

And we can use them to focus on us so that we can do something to help mitigate and prevent the situation that lead to the kinds of anecdotes that we hear.

For instance, when we read about road rage issues, we can work as a community on real problems such as ways to make traffic safer, stop drunk driving, and address the problem of running red lights. Can you have a post-prom party at the teen center to get kids off the road during the danger time, or institute a call-us-for-a-ride service to help inebriated teens. Does your street corner need a stop sign? At the same time, we can work as individuals to make our own driving better.

It is obvious that for each category of Life Rage, we need to combat it by focusing on both individual and community solutions, the ones where we join with others and enlist government, schools, churches and other resources in the outside world—the civic arena. William Bennett has said that "our cultural virus has created its own antibodies. People are fighting back to reclaim their children, their culture, and their country. There are a number of things we can do to encourage cultural renewal. Our greatest hope lies in our social and civic institutions, families, churches, schools, neighborhoods, and civic associations, which have traditionally taken on the responsibility with love, order and discipline.

One such strategy is the Weed and Seed approach used in some communities meant to stabilize conditions in poorer neighborhoods. Under the Department of Justice, Weed and Seed provides an overall collective aim for disparate programs—a way to coordinate and plan an activity that is meant to serve an incubator for social change and to promote restoration. The Weeding part is to concentrate and enhance enforcement efforts to identify, arrest and prosecute violent offenders, drug traffickers and other criminals, to "eliminate the negative" from a target area.

Proactive community policing and community engagement lets police officers be assigned to specific locations so that they gain the trust and support of the community. Police and prosecutors work with the resident and businesses as problem-solving partners in law enforcement. Then the seeding can begin, when such human services programs as after school and weekend activities, adult literacy classes and parental counseling are instituted. Federal oversight takes place through the Attorney General's office and is decentralized to reinforce local participation.

Another is the Children's Sabbath project of the Children's Defense Fund. It is a service developed and based on the liturgies and traditions of all the various different faiths and it is meant to involve the adults of the religious congregation in the lives of the children around them, every day of the year, by making them more mindful of the physical, emotional and spiritual needs of the children.

There are many such victories being seen in many areas of life if we only focus on them. One of these is in the balance between family and work. Many companies are striving to provide their employees with what they need to be better spouses, parents, children . . . and workers. For instance:

The Harley-Davidson plant, in York, Pennsylvania, may seem like a strange place for a child care center, but that's where the U-Gro Learning Center is, half a mile from the plant. And 75% of the workers who asked their employer to do something for their kids were men. Next on the docket at the motorcycle manufacturer: a nursing room for mothers.

Another story involves a high-tech start-up in Silicon Valley. (where else?) The management at Centillium, a maker of Internet-access chips, wanted to enlist the families of its workers on its side because it knew the high work load that the employees would be under in the initial phases of the start-up and the toll this would take on workers' families. Centillium threw a big party for the spouses and partners of its workers on a Saturday, telling the workers to stay home and take care of the house and kids so their significant others could be free to party.

The management took care of everything from cutting up

the appetizers to providing each of the workers' mates abut $1000 worth of company stock in their own names (the workers already had their own stock). As a result, the spouses know that while they may be missing having their Centillium employee at home, the absence will result in a positive effect on the family.

Here are some other examples: IBM helped families screen their child care workers in New York and North Carolina in a 1999 pilot program. Texas Instruments sends mobile toy stores to help parents shop for the holidays; Bristol-Myers Squibb lets employees get free baby formula for the first year, mailed in installments. Chase Manhattan Bank offers a backup child-care service for parents whose baby sitter calls in sick or doesn't show up. Eastman Kodak offers elder care backup services and free in-home assessment of elderly dependents.

Nearly 90% of employers let workers take off for school events, and half let them stay home with mildly ill kids without taking sick days, according to a 1998 study by the Families and Work Institute. Yet, only 9% offered child care near the workplace, 33% offered maternity leave after 13 weeks, and 23% offered elder-care resource and referral.

With the rise in adoptions, many companies are giving adoptive parents the same advantages birth parents have in the way of time off for arranging the adoption and staying home with the new child. Some are helping with legal fees and other adoption expenses, in a pattern echoing workplace investment in health benefits that would cover the hospital expenses during birth.

More and more companies allow flex time that gives workers a chance to take care of personal business during the work day if they balance it with time doing company work outside of traditional office hours. This lets workers better balance work time with family time.

We must all also begin to work to overcome the myths of family life. The family is not disintegrating, despite rumors to the contrary. The family is alive and well in America, with fathers taking on more responsibility for the children. In 1998, for instance, 40% of dads said that they believed child care was a joint responsibility.

Most families function enough on some level. Not all families function perfectly all the time—what does?—and not all are totally dysfunctional. Plus, the effect of any family on a particular child will be different depending on the child.

This generation, statistically, when you get beyond the anecdotes, is about as good or bad as former ones, with the same percentages involved in welfare services or the justice system. Most kids grow up in families and communities that enable them to do reasonably well as adults. We must balance our need to help those kids who are at risk with the knowledge that we are raising a lot of good kids. And we need to find out what there is about how our good kids are being raised so that we can use the information to help the others.

## ALL IN THE FAMILY

Some of what we know about how to raise good kids in good families is well known and has been for a long time, but it never hurts to repeat it for those who may not have gotten the message in this generation. Begin taking charge of your household, reasserting your parental authority, and disciplining your children. Co-ed sleepover? Just say no. If you do not provide the rules, your child will turn to his tribe of peers for structure and a sense of family.

It has to be done on a family by family basis. When I was working as a patrol officer for the Akron Police Department, we were responding to a neighborhood burglary. My assignment was to go door to door and see if anyone witnessed any suspicious people and/or cars in the neighborhood.

I went to several homes, and in one, I noticed that the residence was dirty, with dirty dishes in the living room tables, newspapers on the floor, dirt on the floors and several kids running around screaming while I was attempting to interview the mother. Once of the children came up to me and interrupted our conversation several times, with the mother saying nothing to these screaming and disrespectful kids.

I then went next door. The mother at this residence opened the door and said, "Good evening, officer, how can I help you?" I explained that we were conducting neighborhood interviews since we had a burglary. This very pleasant woman invited me in her home. Once inside the door, I observed a clean and orderly home. She asked if she could get me a fresh glass of water.

Her three children came running down the steps towards me. Once these children were standing in the living room where I was standing, the mother told the children to sit on the couch while this nice officer talked. Immediately, these three children sat on the couch and they were some of the most pleasant and polite kids I have ever encountered on my police job.

I asked myself all night how could two homes next to each other in the ghetto have such a difference physically and why the children differed from each other so much. One home evidently was showered with the right combination of love and discipline, and against all odds it made a difference!

Here's an example from my own life of what I mean about raising kids, and it is about setting a good example. When my son Darrin was six, I promised on a Monday evening that we would watch the Cleveland Browns that next weekend while feasting on cheese snacks and root beer. All week long, he was after me to buy the snacks, and when I brought them home, he guarded them from the rest of the family until the magic day arrived. Today, Darrin and I still enjoy the root beer and cheese snacks tradition during football games and other sports. But what if I had had beer while he drank the root beer? It's not that parents can't have a cold beer in front of their kids. But seeing that six-pack every time he opens the refrigerator will let a kid know that drinking is just a matter of course. The same goes for coaches smoking cigarettes. You must model the behavior you want your children and the athletes you coach to have.

Discipline does not mean just punishment, although appropriate punishment for wrongdoing is a part of it. But the word discipline derives from a Latin word for learning, and it is related to the word disciple and to the idea of a discipline in the academic sense. Discipline really means teaching, and that is essentially what parents do, from teaching the baby to walk to teaching the teen why certain behaviors are a bad idea. Many times, this means making sure that their actions, good or bad, have natural and logical consequences. It also means engendering a sense of responsibility in your children and requiring them to contribute in some way to both family life and to the community at large.

Don't just pile up self-esteem on a kid without giving him or her a chance to earn it. Pay attention to your child and praise him when you catch him doing right, and teach him how to do things. If you do not pay attention to your child for the positive things he or she does, the child will start looking for other ways to gain your attention and that of others, be they tattoos, nose rings, criminal activity or the like. Indeed, even outside the family, it is important to reward positive works, find someone who is doing something right and tell him or her so, with appreciation.

Chores are a perfect example of what kids need to do. One mother in Minneapolis has a very bright little daughter, and the kid knows how to swim, play violin, paint, and write haiku. She takes lessons from dawn to dusk and is never allowed to be alone with an unstructured minute. But she has not learned how to do housework and has no home responsibilities, for her mother believes that this kind of work is beneath a liberated woman, which she wants her daughter to be.

But all adults live in households and all should learn the basics of how to make a household run when they are boys and girls, from grocery shopping to cooking to cleaning to yardwork. Kids need to feel competent and to know that they are contributing. Learning chores at a parent's side is also a good way to pass along knowledge from generation to generation, as well as stories from the past. It's a good time to talk. This knowledge will be sorely needed before the kid goes to college and can't make a bed or do laundry. So we have a list of regular, age-appropriate chores the child is responsible for as a natural part of family life.

As parents, my wife Michelle and I have tried to do the right things for our three children. So, early in their childhood years, we created a home work chart that listed three sets of jobs that were required each week by each of our three children. This work chart would rotate each week, thus changing the jobs assigned, so that some weeks the child might get a harder task or one that they enjoyed more. Regardless, the rotation kept it fair for all three children. Additionally, they had to do their work assignment, such as running the sweeper, a minimum of three times a week. Each time they completed the task, they had to check off one of the three squares by their name. If, and ONLY if they completed their work assignment and checked off the three squares by their name did they get paid their weekly allowance. The simple reward was a low weekly allowance— and appreciation for your food and clothing.

I remember one of my children asking me whether, if they did two out of three jobs, they would still get paid a portion of their allowance. My response was, "If you agree to help someone, work for someone or do a homework assignment, and you only do part of it, you are not completing your end of the deal and therefore you do not deserve any reward for your efforts." I further explained that full commitment and full completion of all tasks in life is very, very important and would separate one from the rest. It was at that point that I realized that this home structure of work assignments had far-reaching effects for their future, and I was glad we decided to do it early in their lives.

In addition, self-esteem without self-control is just selfish. One lesson kids need to learn is how to control their exuberance into well-mannered behavior and how to control their basic, infant self-centeredness as they grow up by learning to think about others.

If we want a family life, we actually have to create a family life that will make us something more than a collection of individuals living in the same house. Dinner time is a perfect place to do this. It is said that two-thirds of Americans eat dinner while watching TV. So turn it off and talk. Use dinnertime as a chance to teach manners and the art of polite conversation. Ask the kids specifics about their day, not just general "How's it going?" questions. Come to the table with observation about your own day to prime discussion. Or declare a topic of the day. Have a discussion about cuisines of other cultures or regions and try one or two new dishes every once in a while to stimulate discussion about how others live. Encourage kids to participate in meal preparation and clean up as a group activity. Invite your kids' friends to come over as well as adult friends who will make it a company meal. Teach social skills and the ability to interact. Make dinner a pleasant time without overwhelming discipline and attention to what's being eaten. And consider having breakfast or brunch on a weekend if an evening meal is impossible.

*The late Ann Landers published a column that had a list of a dozen suggestions to parents from their kids in the Dothan (Alabama)* Eagle. *It is often requested to be republished. Perhaps this is because it includes some good advice:*

1. Don't give me everything I ask for. Sometimes I am just testing you to see how much I can get. (Or you can find ways to help your child earn what he needs or wants)
2. Don't always give orders. Sometimes I will respond better to a suggestion than a command.
3. Don't keep changing your mind about what you want me to do. Make up your mind and stick to it. In other words, be consistent.
4. Keep promises, both good and bad. It you promise a reward, give it to me, and the same with punishments.

5. Don't compare me with anyone else. It leads to hurt feelings.
6. Let me do as much for myself as I can. That's how I learn. If you do it, I will never learn to do it for myself.
7. Don't correct my mistakes in front of others.
8. Don't scream at me. It makes me want to scream back.
9. Don't tell lies in front of me and ask me to do so to help you out.
10. When I do something wrong, don't ask me to tell you why I did it. I don't always know why I did it.
11. Don't pay too much attention to my minor physical problems. Make sure my illnesses are real before you let me out of doling something based on them.
12. Treat me like you would a friend, with respect and politeness.

The latter is a key issue. Often, adults brush in front of children in public places as if they weren't there. Kids can only learn politeness and good manners if these traits are demonstrated to the kids.

Children must learn accountability for their own actions and discipline that will enable them to take the right actions. In children and in others, we must stop tolerating irresponsible behavior. People can be irresponsible through ignorance, habit or choice. When you feel it is wise, a gentle word may let someone else know that certain behaviors are unacceptable. Focus on the behavior, not the person.

If a person is rude, be it your child or a stranger, and you can tell he or she is having a bad day, you can often turn around his or her mood with humor or an understanding approach. You can sometimes meet the anger in others, not with a lecture or by becoming angry in turn, but by a sympathetic outpouring. Be patient with an annoying person rather than letting that person hook you into your own life rage. And reach out to those who need comfort.

Kids who do not learn the lessons of life in pleasant and easy ways as a part of family interaction may have to learn them in a harder way, and no parent would prefer that. However, some parents are forced to turn to tough love programs for very troubled teens that involve taking the kids out in handcuffs sometimes and taking them to behavior modification camps that use solitary confinement and restraints.

However, some advocates say that kids need to be protected from such programs. A recent case in Columbus, Ohio, found Barbara and Scott Goen in trouble for sending their son Justin, a school drop-out and substance abuser, off to such a camp. The Department of Child Services in the community stepped in to monitor the treatment, which required Justin to ask permission even to go to the bathroom to overcome his overwhelming sense of unearned entitlement. It also required study, chores, physical education and adherence to strict rules. Justin believes he was helped by the program, saying he earned a GED degree, motivation, confidence in himself and a new appreciation for his family.

In addition to safeguarding kids from their own inexperience and immaturity by teaching them to control their own emotions and behavior, we must also guard from others who would do them harm. Some of these are found in the electronic media and the Internet. We can never just use these as electronic babysitters for there is too much in there we cannot expose our children to and other things they might need us sitting by to explain and to put into perspective.

Other terrors are closer to home and in the physical world. There are many adults we rely on to teach our kids skills and interact with them to expose them to a wide variety of personality types, ideas and beliefs. But we have to be sure to monitor the kids by looking at their youth leaders such as music teachers, coaches, scout leaders and even Sunday-school teachers. Don't turn these coaches or tutors or whatever into baby sitters for you while you go about your adult business. This is partly for your kids' sake to protect them and partly for the benefit of the youth leaders, because they are there to teach your child that special skill and not to parent your child. Make sure schools and extracurricular programs do background checks on these persons. Don't fall for flattery about how talented your child is that is calculated to win your blind trust.

Talk to your child about time spent with the teacher or coach or scout leader and make sure the child knows he or she can be honest about what is going on without leading them into unwarranted suspicion. Beware of any gifts the coach or teacher is giving your child. Stay informed about road trips and how much free time is available. Ask about rooming, dressing and bathing situations.

## THE WORKPLACE

There are also strategies that an individual can use in the workplace to help overcome work rage and to better balance work with family life. First, you can think of all of your life as a game in which you are juggling balls, work, family, health, friends and spirit. Think of work as a rubber ball when all the rest are glass and will shatter if dropped.

It will also help to think of your work more positively, as a way to use your own skills to make a contribution, as well as a way to be independent and self-sufficient. Try to look at the bigger picture. There is an old story of seventeenth-century England. Three workmen were approached and asked what they were doing. The first responded in a surprised tone, "Why, any fool can see I am setting stone." The second answered angrily, "I am earning a shilling a week [or whatever the rate was then]." The third said proudly, "I am helping Sir Christopher Wren build a great cathedral."

Work in concert with others in recognition that the work is interdependent. Why not have a thank-God-it's-Monday party to realize that the work has a purpose and enables you to produce something and to use your skills? Some think of their work as a sacred activity as it lets them cooperate with others to create and sustain goods and services in behalf of others.

Another key is to look at the office bulletin board. There is no secret as to why all those Dilbert cartoons are on cubicle walls. Humor is one of the best ways to deal with stress in any area and especially at work. In a 1999 William Mercer poll, 8% of respondents said that language about having fun at work was part of their mission statement. Almost two-thirds said they think having fun at work benefits employees and the organization as a whole. It reduces stress, improves creativity, creates loyalty, improves job satisfaction, and promotes better customer service, and even improves productivity.

Peter Drucker suggests also that managers think beyond the daily grind and its challenges and focus instead on cosmic terms. Take a new look at management practice such as teams— not a bad idea in themselves, and in fact a dandy idea, but only if the information flows two ways and not just from the top down, so that managers continue to learn from those in the front lines just what the company should be doing to serve customers.

Employers are now beginning to turn to younger workers and states are trying aggressively to keep their college graduates in the state. Georgia, Florida and Maryland have programs in place. And some temp agencies are looking at younger workers for high-tech summer jobs by offering them cash bonuses, lotteries for prizes and training.

Think of periods of unemployment as a chance to look for new routes to happiness at work. Decide what you are good at, build on those strengths, and try to decide what you really want to be when you grow up based on this assessment. Use the chance to design a new career tailored to you. At the same time, look for weaknesses and identify the ones that stand in the way of what you want to accomplish, and then overcome them. For instance, if you are afraid to speak in public and it would help you get to where you want to be, join Toastmasters and do something about it. If your weaknesses are immaterial, stop focusing on them.

## Pursue Simplicity

Overcoming Life Rage takes a community approach to solving problems as well as new ways of dealing with the family and with work. But part of it begins in the human heart as well, within the individual. It will entail some overall new strategies and ways of thinking, a new way to look at life in all areas, at work, at school and at home, on the road and in the air, in the civic, governmental and business arenas. Avoiding Life Rage means that we should be more positive and grateful, become outwardly instead of inwardly directed, and learn to deal better with change. Above all, take hold of and retain your spiritual side.

For many people, overcoming Life Rage begins by choosing simplicity. People often work to simplify their lives after events such as birth, illness, death or a job change. Some 15% of baby boomers are actively choosing a simpler life, according to Trends Research Institute. More will join them.

Reduce materialism by buying things consciously, being aware of the cost of maintenance. Move away from a high-speed, high-demand lifestyle and stop the merry-go-round. A slower lifestyle improves your mental and physical health. Have a lowered sense of achievement and stop asking so much of yourself and your career. Build customer and supplier relationships over time. Have extended conversation with neighbors on the porch or the store and build communities.

A preacher for the Discovery Church focused on this in a recent sermon. Society, he said, has given us fast food that we do not even have to leave the car to get it, as well as video monitors on shopping carts so no time need be lost. It is all what he calls part of Hurry Disease, when we try to do all kinds of things, acquire all kinds of things. He reminded his listeners of the little boy who asked his father why he brought home his briefcase every night. "Because I can't get all the work done at the office," answered the father. "Then why," said the little boy, used to the first grade way of doing things like apportioning kids to reading groups, "don't you ask them to put you in a slower group?"

It's a good idea. In life, says the preacher, more needs to become enough. We must stop always going after mass quantities—of possessions, of accomplishments, of money, of experience—and know that what we have suffices to fill our needs, and that our needs must be met in spiritual ways. We must learn contentment, no matter what, he says, so that we have no sense of need and no need of haste.

## BECOME POSITIVE

Expect that good things will happen. Optimism pays, it is known, because the things that you focus on will increase and the things you disregard tend to diminish.

Teddy Roosevelt has a brother Elliott and both were born into wealth. Teddy, who was a sickly youth, worked for health and lived a long, active life, while his brother, the golden-haired boy, died a failure at 34.

Positive psychology is a new way of helping people to live better. According to clinical research, optimists have better immune systems, mental agility and are more creative. Even HIV positive patients, whom most persons would not regard as lucky, had a correlation between their degree of optimism and level of symptoms, which in turn had an effect on the kind of care they took of themselves.

Eliminate the negative aspects in your life, be they toxic people or the little annoyances like that sticky door handle that needs to be fixed and oiled.

## SHOW GRATITUDE

With all this comes a need to express gratitude for even the smallest of blessings. Express gratitude for what you have rather than wanting always more. One message I was e-mailed put it well:

- I am thankful for the mess to clean after a party, because it means I have friends.
- I am thankful for the taxes I pay because it means I am working.
- I am thankful for the snug fit of my clothes, because it means I have clothes and enough food to eat.
- I am thankful for a lawn that needs mowing and windows that need washing and gutters that need fixing because it means I have shelter.
- I am thankful for all the complaining I hear about the government because it means I have free speech.
- I am thankful for my heating bill because it means I am warm.
- I am thankful for the far away spot I found in the parking lot because it means I can walk.
- I am thankful for the piles of laundry and cooking I do because it means my loved ones are near and I can provide for them.
- I am thankful for aching muscles at the end of a day because it means I have been productive.
- I am thankful for the lady behind me in church who sings off key because I have freedom of religion.
- I am thankful for the alarm in the early morning because I am alive.

## DEVELOP OUTWARD THINKING

Life requires us all to rely on others and to let others rely on us. Be sure to create a team of family and friends that will help you out emotionally and even financially when the going gets rough. But in order to be able to rely on your team, you have to let them know that they can rely on you.

Do something unselfish for someone each day. It needn't be a big deal—just a kind word or small favor. Scrap off your neighbor's windshield after a snowstorm, for instance. It's all part of a campaign we've recently based on a movie called *Pay It Forward*, where people do favors for each other before they need to pay it back. Others have called it Random Acts of Kindness and Senseless Beauty.

Leave the world a little better than you found it. Hikers know that if you pack it in, you have to pack it out. But go a little farther and do a little more. Pick up the litter as you go by. Keep a grocery bag and maybe a pair of gloves in the car for this purpose. And it's not even such an unselfish thing—you can easily lose weight and get in shape by doing this. At the same time, you can minimize your own pollution by recycling, reusing, reducing what you use and buying recycled goods.

Be appreciative of others, in whatever role in your life, from spouse to store clerk, and be sure to thank them, especially those who work for you.

Make sure your kids learn this as well. Kofi Annan, the Secretary General of the United Nations, suggest that kids can make the world better by getting to know people whose lives are different than theirs. Find out why they do what they do and what you have in common with them. This is how to avoid raising kids with the kind of xenophobia that can lead to Life Rage.

This learning to be other-centered works in schools as well. Students in automotive repair program at Lincoln Technical Institute in Columbia, Maryland, work on donated cars that are later sold for the cost of the repair parts to former welfare recipients entering the job market under a program called Cars for Careers. This helps both the student learners and the newly employed people who need transportation to their jobs and interviews.

Find out what your special talent is and use it. Is it a craft, the written word, a skill in games or athletics? Emma Grafton, an octogenarian in Butler, Pennsylvania, gets donations of scraps and makes them into nine-by-nine-foot quilts—some 50 a year.

Finally, when you see something you think is wrong, get together with others who feel the same way, and take action on the problem. Small steps count. Add your voice to others by becoming informed about issues and then speaking up. It's getting easier with e-mail and voice mail.

## Accept Change

You must learn to accept change as a fact of life, as life is a process of becoming used to learning new ways and ideas. Change is an opportunity to let life take you in a new direction. If you do so, it may surprise you and even delight you. Try to take life less personally. If your employer criticizes your work, fix the work. If another driver needs to get ahead of you, let him.

Be yourself. Don't compare yourself to others. Your uniqueness is what makes you special. Don't set your goals by what others tell you. Know that many in life will disagree with you and some people will not like you. Know what is most important to you and don't take for granted the most important things to you.

Know that change, even positive change, is stressful and that it can affect your health, so you must safeguard it. Stressors can be positive things like a promotion, move, marriage or a holiday. Conflict may arise from a need to get attention, so try to give positive attentions before the negative ones can emerge.

There is a lot of evidence that anger and rage are risk factors for heart disease and for stroke in both sexes. Anger thickens the walls of the arteries, and health care workers know that much illness is psychosomatic in nature, when the thoughts of the brain lead to feelings that affect the body.

These findings suggest that you can't just learn to manage anger, but to prevent it, by accepting conflict as a normal part of life. Some stress, which really just translates to change, is good. You cannot live without some stress. Things such as aggression, depression and addiction may not be caused by stress by but a lack of it, by boredom, a lack of something that engages you. You need something to live for as well as to live on. You need meaning as well as the means to live.

Calm your physical self with scents, candles, hot water soaks. Meditate to give yourself a chance each day to be calm. If you have never taken to sitting down to meditate, try something like tai chi that lets you move and gives your mind something to engage itself other than the old rat race.

At the same time, learn to relax your adult responsibilities by regaining some of the childlike wonder of the world. Play kick ball. Ride a bike. Climb a tree. Paint with finger paints. Lie under a tree and drink lemonade. Enjoy M&Ms. Get excited about little things. Do these things with your kids.

Deal with change by becoming more creative. Engage in rituals to give you a sense of stability and a secure place to stand by performing a task or a celebration in the same way and at the same time every day, week or year. Rituals can be found in the events of daily life: food, clothing, bathing, even housework.

You can create a ritual in the act of pouring a cup of tea before you sit down to work or by writing in a journal before bedtime. And the journal will also serve the purpose of letting you keep track of where you have been, a key factor in dealing with change.

## SEEK THE SPIRITUAL

Many people in our culture today are prone to hostility, are living on the edge of resentment, are demonstrating violent attitudes toward others and even toward themselves. Some of these folk are ready to explode. We all need to get in touch with our deepest emotions, including rage, and find a way to experience healing and reconciliation. This book you are reading now includes several worthwhile suggestions for developing further our physical, mental, and emotional capacities. However, paying attention to these significant dimensions is not enough. We need to tap into the spiritual dimension of being human which undergirds and weaves together all other aspects of who we are.

Let's look at two different individuals in a simple fable. John was in his 40s and angry at the world. He was resentful toward his two oldest children who had moved out of state. He believed they should have stayed closer to their family roots. His job was a source of anguish because of never receiving a promotion he felt he deserved. He grumbled often about being in his 40s, adding that the rest of his life was all downhill.

Esther lived to be 100 years old. She had experienced many hardships and hurts in her life that could have festered into a lifelong bitterness and resentment. Esther's husband had abandoned her many years before, her daughter developed a serious illness which brought her to a premature death, and her son lived at a great distance and was not able to visit her as often as they both desired. However, she was a woman of joy and peace who, even in her late '90s, was visiting nursing homes to read poetry and tell personally composed stories to the residents.

What made the difference in attitude between John and Esther? Clearly, the difference between these two people was not that John had experienced greater misfortunes in life. Rather, it was their divergent outlooks on life. John viewed life as a battle against the world conflict, a no-win situation. Esther's perspective on life fostered in her a sense that life is a precious gift, that difficulties along the way were learning experiences and reminders of her dependency on God and others, that one's purpose in life is to serve others and make a positive difference in the world.

Esther looked at and responded to life from a deeply spiritual point of view. Her own understanding of God, the foundation of her interior life, gave her a strong sense of identity and security as a beloved child of God. No person or circumstance could take that away from her. She did not believe that God caused bad things to happen. She trusted that God could work through all circumstances and bring good out of them. Esther felt in her heart that the Lord would never abandon her. Her inner strength came not only from her own energy but from tapping into the power of the living God. She was able to forgive her husband for abandoning the family because of her own experience of God's unconditional love and mercy. Growing older for Esther was an opportunity to grow wiser, to be more deeply grounded upon her spiritual foundation, to continue to fulfill her life purpose—bringing a little goodness to others.

Consider the words of Darrell Scott, the father of Columbine student Rachel Scott, a man who has faced an overwhelming trauma yet kept faith in God. Before the House of Representatives Judiciary subcommittee, he said, "We all contain the seeds of kindness and the seeds of violence. The death of my wonderful daughter, Rachel Joy, and the death of that heroic teacher and the other eleven children who died must not be in vain. Their blood cries out for answers.

"The first recorded act of violence was when Cain slew his bother Abel out in the field. The villain was not the club he used. Neither was it the NCA, the National Club Association. The true killer was Cain, and the reasons for the murder could only be found in Cain's heart.

"Men and women are three-part beings. We all consist of body, soul and spirit. When we refuse to acknowledge a third part of our makeup, we create a void that allows evil, prejudice and hatred to rush in and wreak havoc. Spiritual influences were present without our educational systems for most of our nation's history. Many of our major colleges began as theological seminaries. This is a historical fact. What has happened to us as a nation?

"There is a spiritual awakening taking place that will not be squelched. We do not need more religion. We do not need more gaudy television evangelists spewing our verbal religious garbage. We do not need more million-dollar church buildings built while people with basic needs are being ignored. We do need a change of heart and a humble acknowledgment that this nation was founded on the principle of simple trust in God."

## PRESENCE

As spiritual beings, many people are conscious of an intangible spirit at the depth of who we are—a source of wisdom, strength, virtue, healing, peace, and love. This same spirit awakens us to our essential interconnectedness and interdependency with one another and all creation. People may speak of this spirit as human or divine, as God's Spirit or Holy Spirit or by some other name. We may also be aware, as 12-step programs remind us, that we are to open up our lives to a Higher Power, an Ultimate Reality, a Loving Presence that calls us into a relationship beyond ourselves. This presence, which most people in our culture speak of as God, becomes our fundamental source of meaning and purpose. With faith in God, we are able to view life with all its ambiguity, suffering, and division as still somehow making sense in the grand scheme of things. Each person is called to believe that he or she has a purpose for living, and is called and gifted in some way to make a difference. God is also recognized as the one who guides and empowers us to be people of integrity and love, and who lovingly holds us accountable to do what is right and good.

## PERSPECTIVE

A spiritual orientation toward all of life is a significant factor in dealing with one's own hostility. When we are angry, we need to get a proper perspective on the circumstances in our lives. Sometimes we become upset because another person or circumstance doesn't turn out the way we want. Someone we care deeply about may reject us. A work project we spent months accomplishing may turn out to be a failure. A spiritual perspective reminds us not to turn some other person or situation into the be-all end-all of our lives. No person or accomplishment is meant to be the ultimate in our lives. Letting God be God, our ultimate source of identity and worth, allows us to view everything else in proper perspective. Other people and situations are important, but not so important that we become deeply hostile when circumstances don't turn out the way we desire

We are called to view events through a spiritual lens. No matter what the situation we find ourselves in—whether a traffic jam or losing our job—can we come to believe, like Esther, that we can learn something from this experience? That good can come out of it, and that God will work through it? We may not have the freedom to determine all the circumstances we find ourselves in. But do we believe we have the core freedom to determine how we are going to look at each situation and the attitude we are going to take toward it? As spiritual people, we are called not merely to react to external circumstances, but to live from the inside out being centered in an inner Spirit, in God who is our peace.

## POWER

People today often look to self-help books or programs to change their attitudes, behaviors, and habits. These can certainly be a helpful source for moving in new directions. However, many individuals feel stuck in dysfunctional habits, powerless to change based upon their own self will. Alcoholics Anonymous and other 12-step programs, which have helped to free thousands of lives from enslaving addictions, encourage people to recognize and acknowledge to themselves and others their own powerlessness. Emotions Anonymous, one of the more recent 12-step programs, emboldens participants to openly admit that they are powerless over certain emotions such as anger, and to believe in and turn their will over to a Higher

Power, to the God of their understanding. They are to cooperate with this Higher Power in acknowledging their character defects, admitting these to someone else, and making amends with others, if at all possible.

Such 12-step fellowship groups remind all participants on a regular basis to humbly admit their own ongoing weaknesses and to continue to look to God for strength and guidance one day at a time. The mutual support of group members becomes a source of power through which God can work to transform lives. The importance of fellowship in these programs admonishes us all that we should not try to be Lone Rangers in dealing with destructive emotions such as rage. Each person can open up to a Higher Power or God to ask for and receive encouragement from others.

## PEACE

God, grant me the serenity to accept the things I cannot change . . . so begins the AA Serenity Prayer. People often become hostile because they cannot get their own way. Unmet expectations frustrate many of us. Are we expecting life to be more perfect or secure or pain-free? Do we believe we must please everybody or be thought of by others as a big success? We need to be aware when we are too highly driven by our ego self creating our own frustration because circumstances aren't going exactly as we believe they should. We are called to develop a healthy detachment from our ego self, recognizing that the world is not meant to revolve around us. If there is some aggravation in our lives that we are powerless to change, we ought to be mindful that we can still change our own attitude. We don't have to let other people or circumstances disturb our serenity.

In order to experience deep and lasting peace, it is imperative that we forgive others and ourselves. Realizing that God is the only perfect being, we can let other people and ourselves off the hook for not being perfect. Recognizing that the Lord is willing to forgive anything and everything we have ever done, we are able to pass on his mercy.

Many have found that forgiving others is easier when they remember that all people are wounded in some way. A close friend of mine had a stepfather who was an alcoholic and could be mean spirited. As an adult, he learned that the man's mother had died in childbirth giving him life, and that his father had resented him for that. The stepfather was still responsible for his actions toward my friend as a boy. However, my friend could better understand him and why he acted the way he did. A few years ago, he realized this prayer, and now uses it when relating to difficult people. "Lord, help me to see this person through your eyes and love this person with your heart."

Each of us also needs to see ourselves through God's loving eyes. Knowing that God will still love us regardless, we can more readily admit and deal with our own character defects—not having to rationalize them away or project them onto others. Believing we are forgiven and forgiving others is at the heart of living in love and peace with ourselves and one another.

## PRAYER

We are meant to experience all of life as a communion with God. Taking quiet time to center ourselves, to be more aware of God's ongoing caring and strengthening presence is an important antidote to the frustrations, hurts, resentments, and possible hostilities we may undergo. We need to be receptive to God's breaking into our consciousness at various times throughout the day. Knowing we do not have to deal with every person or circumstance entirely on our own is welcome news. Sometimes I simply pray, "Lord—I need your help [strength, peace, forgiveness, wisdom etc]." Other times I may pray, "Lord—deliver me from my ego self."

I believe that God wants to tell each of us on a regular basis, "Be not afraid. Be not hurt. Be not resentful. I love you and am here to help you. Together, we'll get through this."

# About Timothy A. Dimoff

Timothy A. Dimoff is president of SACS Consulting & Investigative Services, Inc., considered one of the nation's leaders in high-risk workplace management. Available as a speaker, trainer, investigator and author, Dimoff champions for drug-free workplaces and schools and provides integrated human resource solutions for corporations across the nation.

Following 20 years of investigative law enforcement as an Akron, Ohio narcotics detective, Dimoff began SACS Consulting as a means of helping corporations gain control of spiraling workplace crime. He is frequently sought for as a keynote speaker and expert legal witness.

Dimoff's interviews are peppered with dramatic, real-life cases of undercover drug busts, criminal activity, drug-testing scenarios and company turn-arounds after solutions were implemented. He has appeared nationally on radio, television and in major newspapers, including an April 2000 segment on "Stolen Identity" for *Dateline NBC*, a March 2001 segment on CNN for "Workplace 2001 . . . Laid Off and Locked Out" and in several major newspapers including *Chicago Tribune, New York Times, Los Angeles Times* and the *Wall Street Journal*. Topics include: substance abuse and violence prevention, background checks, hair and urine drug testing, stolen identity, on-the-job crime and drug investigations, sexual harassment, employee motivation and anti-drug policies.

Dimoff addresses corporations, schools and parents through six books, including *How to Recognize Substance Abuse, The YOU in Business*, and his new book, "*Life Rage*," a chilling examination of societal rage and safeguards against it.

Winner of innumerable state and local awards for business, safety, leadership and civic achievement, Dimoff and SACS Consulting were awarded the "Weatherhead 100 Award" as one of Ohio's fastest-growing companies. He is a member of the Technical Advisory Services of America, a national expert witness service used by attorneys across the nation; the Ohio and International Narcotic Associations; the Ohio and National Society for Human Resource Managers; and the American Society for Industrial Security.

SACS Consulting Web Page: *www.sacsconsulting.com*
Contact Phone Number: 1-888-722-7937